For Judie,
Sister in Spirit

20 MINUTE KABBALAH

In Warm Friendship
and
In Oneness,

Wayne Dosick

Ellen Kaufman Dosick

20 MINUTE KABBALAH

The Daily Personal Spiritual Practice
That Brings You To
God, Your Soul-Knowing,
and Your Heart's Desires

RABBI WAYNE DOSICK, PH.D.
AND
ELLEN KAUFMAN DOSICK, MSW

 Waterside Publishing

For information: Rabbi Wayne Dosick,
3207 Cadencia, La Costa, CA 92009
1-877 SOUL KID

Waterside Publishing
Cardiff-By-the Sea, California

Interior design: *Carol Freese and David Hadden*
Illustrations: *Carolyn Mickelson*
Cover art: *Gregory J. Balogh*
Cover design: *Chris Stell*
Author photo: *Dennis Davis*

Audio CD: *Cantor Kathy Robbins*
Keyboard: *Tom Laurence*
Recorded at Sea View Sound,
Mark Shapiro

Printed in the United States of America, at Birmingham Press
FIRST EDITION
ISBN 1-933754-50-8 • 978-1-933754-50-5
Library of Congress: 200792

---

20 MINUTE KABBALAH

is a daily personal spiritual practice,

sourced in authentic Tree of Life Jewish mysticism,

that guides you to connect and communicate with God;

to know the essence of your own soul;

and to fulfill the longings of your heart.

It is your pathway to finding answers

to the mysteries of the universe,

and the ultimate questions of human existence.

This engaging, graceful, and deeply satisfying practice,

with its sweet melodies and meditative prayer,

can be done anywhere, any time—

all in just 20 minutes.

For
Joel Fotinos

brother in spirit and Spirit
impassioned messenger of the word and the Word
inspired envisioner of the design and the Design
dear friend

CONTENTS

ACKNOWLEDGMENTS

◆————

מוֹדִים אֲנַחְנוּ
Modim anachu

We are deeply grateful to:

God and Guidance for giving us the sacred task of hearing and bringing down this holy teaching. *"Every day will I bless You, and I will praise Your Name forever and ever."* (Ps. 145:2)

Cantor Kathy Robbins, whose *Yiddisha neshamah*, sweet and compelling voice, and awesome musical talent make the 20 MINUTE KABBLAH CHANTS audio-CD such a work of art and inspiration. And Tom Laurence who accompanies her with such skill and beauty. And Mark Shapiro, at his Sea View Sounds recording studio, whose gentle soul and technological genius weave musical magic.

Rabbinic colleagues and their congregants in synagogues throughout the country who responded with enthusiasm to early versions of the precursor to this work, "Hello, God: Developing a Personal Spiritual Practice."

The members and friends of The Elijah Minyan and the *chavurah* Shir HaYam of Greater San Diego, who have studied with us over the years as we have taught about personal covenant and a deep, intimate relationship with God; and who have *davened* with us as our prayer-chants unfolded into this Kabbalistic *sefirah* spiral.

The members of the first 20 MINUTE KABBALAH class who eagerly and profoundly took in and adopted this practice as their own, and whose wise and loving comments and journals helped shape the current version.

The members of the 20 MINUTE KABBALAH class at Ruach HaAretz–2006, who, from the widest spectrum of Jewish life and observance, embraced the ideas and the practice.

Joel Fotinos, to whom this book is dedicated, who, in wisest counsel and deepest friendship, serves as the "godfather" of this book.

Dr. William Finn, who suggested an early variation of what eventually became the name of the practice and the title of this book.

Stevie Wonder, Carole King, and Judy Chicago, singers of a generation, whose song-words inspire us with prophetic voices and visions.

Colleagues and friends—children of Spirit, each and all—who shared with us their depth of learning; their own spiritual journeys, practices, and commitments; and their wise and good guidance: Rabbi Samuel Barth, Rabbi Ayla Grafstein, Rabbi Diane Elliot, Karen D. Grinfeld, Rabbi Vicki Hollander, Evie Kane, Sharon Jassy, Leo J. Levitt, Rabbi Leah Novick, Deni Phinney, Rabbi Dr. David Posner, Rabbi Jack Riemer, Alan Rubin, Alvin Schultzberg, Rabbi Dr. Yehuda Shabatay, Rabbi Bonnie Sharfman, and, especially, Julie M. Grinfeld, Joseph (Yossi) Adler, and Rabbi Dr. Raachel Jurovics.

Amanda Taylor, whose deep, universal spiritual connection led us to the appropriateness and the power of "The Lord's Prayer."

Carolyn Mickelson, whose deeply Jewish soul and prodigious artistic talent created the illustrations for this book.

Gregory J. Balogh, artist of sweetest soul and inspired hand, whose modern interpretation of the ancient Bush burns with vibrant color and sparks of Light that reveal the Holy Presence.

Deni Phinney, whose kind soul and incredible technological skills helped create the early trial version of the audio CD.

Our mothers, Roberta Dosick, and Anna Kaufman (they should live and be well until 120) and the memory of our holy fathers, Hyman Dosick *zt"l* and Clarence Kaufman *zt"l*, who brought us to God, Torah, and the Jewish people.

Rabbi Shlomo Carlebach *zt"l*, Rabbi Dr. Abraham Joshua Heschel *zt"l* and Rabbi Dr. Zalman Schachter-Shalomi (he, too, along with his beloved Eve, should live and be well until 120) who opened the world of the Spirit to our generation. And Rabbi Dr. Jakob Petuchowski *zt"l*, who taught the perfect balance between mind and heart. And Elie Wiesel (he, too, until 120), conscience out of the ashes, who teaches us to confront, and to wrestle, and to talk, and to shout, and to weep, and to sing, and to listen to the awesome silence. From this world and the Great Beyond, they are our teachers, mentors, and, most of all, our Rebbes.

Our dear friend and "our" priest, the Rev. James J. O'Leary, S.J. (whose Hebrew is good enough to know: *ad meah v'esrim*—"until 120"), who is the living embodiment of holiness, and whose service to God and all of God's children blesses the world.

Rabbi David Cooper and Rabbi Shefa Gold, souls of Spirit, great teachers of Spirit, whose words of blessing grace this book.

William Gladstone, man of vision; agent of Spirit; and with him at Waterside Publishing, Ming Russell—good and kind shepherd.

John Knebels, Carol Freese, David Hadden, and Chris Stell of Birmingham Press—artists of the word; consummate professionals.

And, most, we are profoundly thankful for each other, for the opening to Spirit that we have experienced with each other, and for the great privilege of working and serving with each other in abiding love and daily gratitude.

"The life-dust of Adam was gathered from throughout the entire world."

—BT Sanhedrin 38a

To obtain additional copies of

the 20 MINUTE KABBALAH CHANTS AUDIO CD

by download or on a disk,

and

To learn how you can bring

continuing Kabbalah-learning and practice

into your life,

please visit the website

www.20MinuteKabbalah.com

To invite

RABBI WAYNE DOSICK

to lead a

20 MINUTE KABBALAH

Workshop,

or to invite him to be

Scholar-in-Residence

at your synagogue, church, or in your community,

email: Dosick@20Minute Kabbalah.com

or call

1-877 SOUL KID

הִנֵּנִי

Hineini

Here I Am

PRELUDE

———◆———

Moses stood at the bush.

The bush burned, but it was not consumed.

*And from out of the fire, Moses heard the ever-echoing
Eternal Voice.*

We, too, stand at the bush.

But, for us, it seems to be just a bush.

Where is the flicker? Where is the flame?

*Where is the Voice calling out to us, enveloping us,
summoning us?*

Gently, we talk to the bush, asking for its light.

But, the bush does not burn.

*We sing a song; we chant a wordless melody; we clap our hands,
and dance, and spin around the bush, hoping that our fire will
produce fire.*

Yet, the bush does not burn.

*"Please, God. You spoke to Moses. Now, speak to us. Speak to us
out of the bush. Let us hear Your Voice. Tell us what You want
from us; tell us how we can serve You. Show us our purpose,
our mission."*

1

Silence.
Will we ever see the flame, bask in its glow, be warmed by its fire,
illumined by its light?
Will we ever hear the Voice? Will we ever be called?
More silence.

Maybe it is the wrong bush; maybe we are in the wrong place.
Or, maybe, it is the right bush, but, perhaps, bushes do not burn
anymore. No flame. No Voice.
Or, maybe, we are the wrong people. Who are we to think that we
can come to stand at the bush, yet less hear its Voice?
Or, maybe, it is all just one big story, one big fable, one big myth.
There never was a bush. Moses never stood there. The Voice of
God was never heard.
"Come on, God. If You are there, show YourSelf; prove YourSelf.
Talk to us. At least make the bush burn."

Silence.
Deep, empty silence.
So, we turn to leave.
But, wait.
We cannot go.
The bush will not let us go.
It grasps us in its grip; it holds us tightly in its sway.
The bush claims us.
We belong at the bush.
We belong to the bush.

And, so, we wonder:

*Is there something that we are missing? Is there something that is
eluding us?*

*Are we, perhaps, like those "who have eyes, but do not see; who
have ears, but do not hear"? Like those who hunger, but are not
satiated; whose hearts seek, but have yet to find?*

And, then.

*And, then. At that very moment, in the silence, from the silence—
from the collective unconscious? from the archetypes within?
from God?—comes a soft, murmuring sound, a quiet,
compelling whisper:*

"Be still, and know that I Am."

Ah.

Our deepest soul-memory stirs and awakens.

Now, we remember.

Now, we know.

The bush always *burns;*

The Voice always *speaks*

—if only we open our eyes;

if only we open our ears;

if only we open our hearts.

Silence.

This time, our silence.

The sweetest and most satisfying silence.

The grand silence of great and Eternal knowing.

The bush burns brightly.
We are enveloped in its warmth and bathed in its light.
Holy Sparks emanate from the Holy Presence.
We are breathing in the Divine.
And, like Moses of old, we take off our shoes, and surrender
  our souls.
For, we know that we are standing in a holy place.

BEGINNINGS

◆

The spiritual quest—the search for meaning and purpose in life—is universal.

While religions and faith communities, and individual human beings, have their own unique stories and legends, language and vocabulary, rituals and ceremonies, chants and dances, **the spiritual journey is always the same:** the deep desire to know God; the quest for eternal truth; the search for answers to the mysteries of existence; the need to craft a worthy and worthwhile life; the wish to grow in heart and soul; the yearning for love, for connection, and for Oneness.

Seeking

We come to the bush that holds the Voice from many different places.

Some come as highly intellectual rationalists; others as deeply believing spiritualists. Some are strict legalists; some champion freedom of choice. Some are certain; others doubt. Some are parochial; some are universalists. Some are steeped in history and tradition; others celebrate only the "now moment."

From wherever we come, we know that the rational, scientific, technological world in which we live and work demands a high level of intellectual thought and achievement. We cultivate and honor the world of the mind, and we rejoice when our knowledge and insights lead to greater understanding.

Yet, as human beings, fully involved in the human experience, we hunger for more.

We are, at our core, children of spirit, children of the universe, children of God.

Even as we fully participate in the world of the mind, **the world of Spirit attracts and calls to us.**

Even as we wonder, and, sometimes, wander, we yearn for—or are at least intrigued, or challenged, by—the place where we can encounter God.

We want to be open to the fullness of the universe, to the grand design, to the blueprint for existence.

We want to have access to what is already there, but seems to be hidden from us by the limitations of living on Earth.

We want to be in full connection with the energy and the flow of creation.

We want to remember. We want glimpses of what we once knew, and what, one day, we will know again.

We want to know God—both the transcendent God of the communal covenant, and the immanent God of the "inside of the insides" of our beings.

We want to grow our hearts; we want to grow our souls. We want to grow our "angel wings" as full partners with God.

And, we want to ask God all of our questions—the questions of the ages, the questions of this very moment in time.

Who am I?

From where have I come, and what am I doing here?

How do I best live a life of meaning, a life of worth?

How do I find and sustain true love?

How do I feel deepest happiness, and how do I find and fulfill the grandest desires of my heart?

How do I evolve in mind, in spirit, in consciousness?

Is this all there is?

What happens to me after I die?

Who is God?

Does God have a purpose and a design for the world?

How can a just and loving God permit so much evil and suffering?

Does God have a plan for me? What is my mission? my destiny?

Can I talk to God? Will God talk to me?

In the world of Spirit—through evolving human consciousness— we enter into the gateway that can bring us into the Divine presence.

In the world of Spirit—by means of intuition, night dreams, day dreams, visions, prayer, meditation, chant, body movement, channeling, and soul memory—we move beyond our Earth-existence and Earth-experience, and we open ourselves to receive and hold—if only for a few moments at a time—universal, eternal knowing.

In the world of Spirit, we come to know that there is no separation between us and God, between us and all other human beings; we become vividly aware of the wholeness of existence, the oneness of all peoples.

Yearnings

Whether you are Jewish, Christian, or Muslim, or a follower of an eastern religion, the question is the same: **How shall you nourish your spiritual yearning?**

From the beginning of time until now, religions evolve as the vessels where the questions of existence are asked and answered. Religions are held by communities of faith—where like-minded people join together for prayer, meditation, and study; and for mutal support in facing the grandness and the vicissitudes of life.

It is good to be in faith community—to attend synagogue, or church, or mosque, or temple; to be in the comfortable "at-home-ness" of shared history, friendship, and unity; to know that in communal worship there is collective responsibility, and energy, and power. **In community, there is expression of the communal covenant between God and God's people.**

Yet, the synagogues, churches, mosques, and temples are not as full as they once were.

Our lives—we tell ourselves—are too busy, too hassled, too frenetic. Our jobs, our families, our myriad responsibilities and commitments, and our limited leisure hours, leave us no time for lengthy daily, or even, weekly, worship.

And when we do come to religious services, we may experience the difficulty of trying to truly, devoutly, pray within a structured liturgy, in a large, public, formal group. And we have the deep felt-sense that the religious institutions, like most formal institutions, have a hard time holding the Light of Spirit and God.

And, still, so many of us—you—want to be on the spiritual journey. You want a way to be with the Divine. "Behold, a time is coming when there will be a famine in the land; not a hunger for bread, nor a thirst for water, but for hearing the words of the Lord." (after Amos 8:11)

You want to be at that awesome place where you encounter God— where you are connected and protected, enLightened and loved.

You want to manifest and live your personal covenant with God; to speak not in the "we" of the organized religious collective, but in the deeply individual "I" of intimate relationship. You want that sacred space and those holy moments when you can be nakedly open and honest with your Creator and Sustainer; when you can express your deepest needs and yearnings, your greatest joys and gratitude.

You are a GodSeeker.

You want a spiritual tradition that can be yours; you want to walk a spiritual pathway. You want to be on your SoulJourney.

Kabbalah

One of Judaism's richest, most powerful spiritual traditions, and its mystical pathway to God, and to life's ultimate questions, is Kabbalah.

You may have heard about Kabbalah, especially because of its recent "pop-culture" popularity with contemporary celebrities. But, you may not know much about it.

If you are Jewish, Kabbalah has, perhaps, been hidden from you on the esoteric edges of our faith.

If you are of another religion or faith community—or a spiritual seeker of any kind—Kabbalah has most likely been "too Jewish" and too mysterious for you to explore.

Now as the modern-day interest in "spirituality" has captured the human imagination—fueled in great part by the exploration of eastern religions and Earth-based faith communities—Kabbalah is being rediscovered and embraced.

For, despite its absence from the "mainline" Jewish world for more than the last 250 years; despite its often being dismissed as counter-intuitive to the rational world, and even with the cloak of mystery that still surrounds it, Kabbalistic practice can be a very simple, deeply satisfying endeavor, that can enrich, enhance, and sweeten your life.

Kabbalah is an exquisite pathway to connect and communicate with God, and to delve into the mysteries of the universe and the ultimate meaning of human existence.

The Hebrew word "Kabbalah" means "receive," implying the reception, the access, to the word and will of God.

Kabbalah is a way of looking at the universe beyond what is intellectually known or physically experienced.

Kabbalah is the quest for ultimate meaning.

The practice of Kabbalah centers around:

- study of sacred texts to seek their hidden meanings;
- deep, contemplative meditation as a pathway to God; and
- embracing Kabbalah's teachings that lead to a life of meaning and worth, goodness and right; a life that seeks, in partnership with God, to transform and perfect the world.

Kabbalah is for everyone.

For Jews, it is an opening to the deep places of our collective consciousness. For every spiritual seeker, it is a rich and satisfying pathway for SoulJourney of Spirit.

20 Minute Kabbalah

The teachings of Kabbalah are so boundless, so deeply complex and richly nuanced, so often obscure, enigmatic, and inscrutable—and always so alluring and delicious—that it is tempting to make this book a fully detailed chronicle of the vastness and the potency of the Jewish mystical tradition.

But, this little book has a singular purpose.

Before you can wrestle with the grand mysteries of existence, before you can ask God all your questions, **you have to find God, you have to be with God.**

So, here, we return Kabbalah to its first and most powerful purpose—**to be your mystical pathway to connect and to communicate with God, your own soul-knowing, and your heart's desires.**

Here, we are very happy to introduce you to a sweet, holy, gentle, and highly effective **daily personal 20 minute spiritual practice that gives you the spheric channel to come into deep, intimate relationship with God.**

◆

20 MINUTE KABBALAH

is a daily personal spiritual practice,

sourced in authentic Tree of Life Jewish mysticism,

that guides you to connect and communicate with God;

to know the essence of your own soul;

and to fulfill the longings of your heart.

It is your pathway to finding answers

to the mysteries of the universe,

and the ultimate questions of human existence.

This engaging, graceful, and deeply satisfying spiritual practice,

with its sweet melodies and meditative prayer,

can be done anywhere, any time—all in just 20 minutes.

◆

Riding the Chariot

With authentic Jewish language, rhythms, and chants, 20 MINUTE KABBALAH is rooted in antiquity, and gloriously renews the tradition in our day.

20 MINUTE KABBALAH combines Kabbalah's *merkavah* mysticism with liturgical prayer-text.

Merkavah means "chariot," referring to the chariot in which the biblical prophet Ezekiel rode to the Heavens, holding the vision that the "dry bones" in the valley will once again come to life, as a symbol that Paradise can be both in Heaven and on Earth.

Ezekiel's journey teaches that each and every person—you—can ascend to be in personal contact with God, and that through your relationship with God, Earth can again become Eden—what we call "Sky Blue," the place, the pinnacle, of ultimate perfection.

No less than Abraham, Moses, Isaiah, Ezekiel, and Elijah, **you are a prophet; you can talk to God, and listen when God talks to you.**

In this daily spiritual practice, through the prayers of the liturgy—some old, some newly placed—you can ride your *merkavah* to be with God.

This little book—along with is accompanying audio-CD—can be your companion and your guide.

Here, you will discover:

- the basic principles and purposes of the Jewish mystical tradition
- the new Spiral path in the Tree of Life
- the newly envisioned meaning of the *sefirot,* the steps to God
- 14 simple, melodic chants that take you on your SoulJourney to God
- how to "zoom" your way right into God's holy presence
- how to talk to God
- how to ask God about the secrets of the universe and the mysteries of existence
- how to ask God to fulfill the yearnings of your soul and the desires of your heart

- how to listen as God talks to you
- how to develop and nurture a deep, intimate relationship with God
- how to shape new truths in the Divine Time Tunnel
- how to live in God's Light and EnLightenment
- how to find deep soul-satisfaction and inmost happiness.

And all it takes is just 20 minutes a day!

Why, 20 Minutes?

Why 20 minutes a day?

How can such a powerful spiritual practice take only 20 minutes a day?

Well-understanding the contemporary mindset and heartset—our needs and desires, our constraints and our possibilities—our great teacher and rebbe, Rabbi Dr. Zalman Schachter-Shalomi—one of the great inspirited souls of this generation, and one of this planet's most knowledgeable and fervent universalist ecumenists—says that, in this modern age, "If your suggestions for my spiritual practice exceed twenty minutes in the morning and twenty minutes in the evening, I will not do them, for the old traditions demand more time than I can afford."

The expression of your own individual covenantal relationship with God is not dictated by set time, length, or place—it can be done **anywhere, anytime.** It is not mediated by others, not dependent on anyone else but you and God. It is a way to be in intimate connection with God; to be in private conversation with God; to be gladdened, inspired, and soul-satisfied by your deep bond with God.

In only 20 minutes a day you can come to God and be with God; you can find highest spiritual connection and deepest soul-satisfaction.

Kabbalah For You

Perhaps you already have a rich personal inner prayer-life. 20 MINUTE KABBALAH can enhance it.

Perhaps you attend your place of worship regularly, or even occasionally, but you want something more. You want a short, everyday spiritual practice that can be done anywhere, anytime. 20 MINUTE KABBALAH can be your gateway.

Perhaps you have been wanting to find a way to be with God, but you have been unfamiliar or uncomfortable with the traditional prayers and services. 20 MINUTE KABBALAH can be your "way in."

Perhaps you think that you do not believe, that you lack faith, that you cannot imagine being in relationship with God, that you have no idea how to talk to God or what to say. 20 MINUTE KABBALAH can be your genesis-beginning.

If you would like—as our revered rebbe and teacher Rabbi Shlomo Carlebach *zt"l* (*zecher tzadik l'vrachah:* "May the memory of the righteous be a blessing") used to say—to go to "the highest of the high and the deepest of the deep;" if you would like to immeasurably enrich and ennoble your life, 20 MINUTE KABBALAH is for you.

You can embrace Kabbalah.
Kabbalah can work for you.
Through the mystical pathways of Kabbalah,
you can enter into God's holy Presence,
talk to God,
listen while God talks to you,
wrestle with the questions of eternity,
find deep soul-satisfaction, and the inmost happiness of your heart,
and become a more enLightened being—
all in just 20 minutes a day.

———◆———

20 MINUTE KABBALAH

FAST-TRACK

If you want to have a bit of background

in the history, texts, concepts, and practice of Kabbalah;

and if you would like to learn our theory of the evolution

of Kabbalah

to this very moment in time,

we invite you to read the next three chapters,

"Kabbalah 101," "The New Tree of Life," and

"Spiraling to God."

If you would rather begin your 20 MINUTE KABBALAH

spiritual practice immediately,

please turn directly to

"20 MINUTE KABBALAH—HOW IT WORKS,"

which begins on page 43.

———◆———

We are pleased to invite you into the wondrous world of Kabbalah. We are privileged to invite you to come to the bush that always burns. We are honored to invite you on your SoulJourney to God.

KABBALAH 101

—◆—

With roots stretching back to the Bible and nurtured throughout Jewish history, Kabbalah began to grow and flourish with the publication of *The Zohar—The Book of Splendor.*

Tradition attributes the *Zohar* to the second-century rabbinic sage Shimon bar Yochai. Modern scholarship argues that the real author is Moses de Leon of 13th century Spain, who attempted to make the reader think that bar Yochai was the writer, thus giving the *Zohar* historical roots and authenticity.

Either way, beginning in the 13th century, the new Kabbalists shifted Judaism away from the philosophical rational—championed earlier by the 12th century sage Moses Maimonides—into the spiritual. In the long history of Jewish thought—which, pendulum-like, continually swings between coming to God through faith, and attempting to explain God through reason—faith was once again ascendant.

The Zohar brings down mystical teachings on the five books of the Torah, emphasizing that God—and by extension every human being who is created "in the image of God"—holds both male and female attributes; that in addition to the communal covenantal relationship, there is a deep, personal, intimate relationship between each and every person and God; that there are higher truths beyond the literal, or even moral, meaning of the biblical text; that every human act has a continuing ripple effect on the entire universe—and, surely, on God;

and that the highest goal of a human being is to reach for and try to understand the innermost secrets of existence.

In the 16th century, the center of Kabbalah study and practice moved to the city of S'fat (Safed) in the north of Israel.

In the 18th century, the emerging Chasidic movement of Eastern Europe, Russia, and Ukraine deepened Kabbalistic meditation with ecstatic prayer and joyous chants and dance.

Because Kabbalah dips into the esoteric, by custom, its study and practice has been limited to the "initiated"—that is well-learned, emotionally stable, married Jewish males over the age of 40. Until the Chasidim, Kabbalah was never given over to the Jewish masses, and was most-always shrouded in an aura of veiled secrecy.

The Emancipation and the Enlightenment of the last 250–300 years—most-characterized by the embrace of rational, intellectual thought—sent Kabbalah into the shadows, and pushed it to the "fringes" of Jewish life, where it was largely ignored and essentially dismissed.

As the great modern sage, Rabbi Aryeh Kaplan *zt"l* explained, "Until the rise of the Jewish Enlightenment, mysticism and intellectualism had equal status within Judaism. The ostensible goal of the Enlightenment was to raise the intellectual level of Judaism . . . [but] it was often at the expense of other Jewish values. The first values to fall by the wayside were Jewish mysticism. . . . Anything that touched upon the mystical was denigrated as superstition and occultism. . . ."

Now, in recent days, Kabbalah has surged up from the Jewish underground, and has been hailed as the Jewish channel into the world of Spirit.

Finding God

In order to best utilize Kabbalah as our SoulJourney pathway to God, it is helpful to understand some of Kabbalah's fundamental teachings.

Us

Kabbalah teaches that we live in Four Worlds.

1. Physical—Doing

2. Emotional—Feeling

3. Mental—Knowing

4. Spiritual—Being.

Although these worlds may seem linear—stretching from the physical upward to the spiritual—they are actually all interconnected and interdependent. Their fully integrated and unified coexistence is the fullness and the wholeness of our beings.

We live in—we are—all Four Worlds simultaneously.

The whole of existence is in each and every individual existence. Each and every personal world is the whole world.

When we put ourselves into the world of Spirit, we enter with our entire selves, our entire beings, the totality of our Four Worlds. We balance body, heart, mind, and soul. We journey from this three dimensional world in which we live, toward the fifth dimension and beyond, where we can be in full oneness with God.

We become the meeting point where Heaven and Earth touch.

God

Kabbalah calls God *Ein Sof,* meaning "Without End"—"Infinite."

By calling God *Ein Sof,* Kabbalah indicates that God is the Everything of the Everything, the Everywhere of the Everywhere. God has no limitation, no boundaries, no delimited role.

At the same time, Kabbalah affirms the biblical teaching that "The candle—the spark, the light, the flame—of God is the soul of human beings." (Prov. 20:27)

That which animates us and gives us life is the breath and the light of God. We are living human beings because we each have a part of God within us.

Unlike God, we have boundaries that are imposed upon us by the limitations of our physical bodies.

But, our souls have no limitations. They can traverse the universe, from being here in the physical world of Earth, to being with God in merged union.

Connecting

Kabbalah teaches that the way to come to the place where Heaven and Earth meet, the way to journey between the Infinite and the finite, the way for us to reach God, and for God to reach us, is by means of ten emanations, or steps, called *sefirot.* (singular: *sefirah)*

The Journey

The *sefirot*—which hold the characteristics and attributes of God— are the steps that emanate from God to the Earthly world, in descending order; and are, at the very same time, the steps that are the pathways from us to God, in ascending order. They are like rungs on a ladder that connect Heaven and Earth—God and human beings— and, they reflect to human beings, who are created "in the image of God," the Godly characteristics and attributes to imitate.

As we human beings imitate God's *sefirotic* attributes, the *sefirot* become filled with our human energy, and we and God reflect each other. We look into the *sefirot* and see God; God looks into the *sefirot* and sees us.

The early Kabbalists named and defined ten (in practice, twelve) *sefirot.*

Each *sefirah* has its own individual attributes and energy—both God's and ours. On the journey to God, every part, all the parts together—each and every *sefirah*—is needed as an integral part of the whole.

The Kabbalists visualized these *sefirot* in a structured order, or form, yet each *sefirah* relates to all the others through matrix lines of connection.

They called the interconnected design of the *sefirot* The Tree of Life.

The *sefirot*—their traditional names, translations, and definitions, and in their traditional ascending order, from Earth to Heaven—are:

1. **MALCHUT. "Kingdom."** The place of union between God and humankind—the place where the Infinite and the finite meet on Earth.

   This *sefirah* is also known as **SHECHINAH, "The InDwelling Presence,"** the feminine attributes of God—the place where the masculine and the feminine of God, the wholeness of God, blend, and where human beings, created in the image of God, become aware of the "everything of the everything."

2. **YESOD. "Foundation."** The life force; the harmonizer and the synthesizer; the balancer of nature.

3. **NETZACH. "Victory; Endurance."** The energy of expansion and growth.

   and its partner:

4. **HOD. "Glory."** The energy of reigning in and limitation.

5. **TIFERET. "Beauty."** The anchor; the heart-seat of truth; the place of equilibrium.

6. **CHESED. "Lovingkindness."** The place of deepest love and widest compassion.

   and its partner:

7. **GEVURAH. "Strength."** The place of discernment and restraint. This *sefirah* is also known as **DIN, "Judgment,"** the place of mediation between right and wrong.

> **There is a "shadow" *sefirah*, which is actually two *sefirot*—**the entrance (back) and the exit (front) to what is best described as "God's Time Tunnel." These *sefirot* are part of the Tree of Life, yet not fully.
>
> 8. **DA'AT. "Knowledge." The entering.**
>
> 9. **DA'AT. "Knowledge." The emerging.**

10. **CHOCHMAH. "Wisdom."** The place of perception; thought; intuition.

and its partner:

11. **BINAH. "Understanding."** The place of feeling; experience.

12. **KETER. "Crown."** The place where God dwells; where human beings go up to meet God; the place of illumination and revelation.

The *sefirot* are in three columns.

The central column—which is the anchor—holds *Malchut, Yesod, Tiferet, and Keter,* and the shadow *sefirot* of *Da'at.*

The left side—which is the feminine side—holds *Hod, Gevurah,* and *Binah.*

The right side—which is the masculine side—holds *Netzach, Chesed,* and *Chochmah.*

The traditional image of the Tree of Life looks like this.

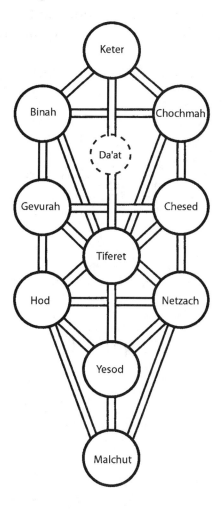

Because we are looking at the image of the Tree of Life from the front, it seems as if the right side is the left side, and the left side is the right side.

But, actually, we are looking at the image standing directly behind it, and so right and left are really right and left.

The right—which is the masculine—is giving, expanding, initiating.

The left—which is feminine—is receiving, contracting, embracing.

The right is the OutBreath; the left is the InBreath of continuing creation.

The Kabbalists wanted the *sefirot* to be totally accessible to us; they wanted us to be able to viscerally feel their place and their purpose. They especially wanted us to be fully conscious of the supporting central column, and of the role of the feminine and masculine.

So, they superimposed the *sefirot* of the Tree of Life onto human form. The image looks like this.

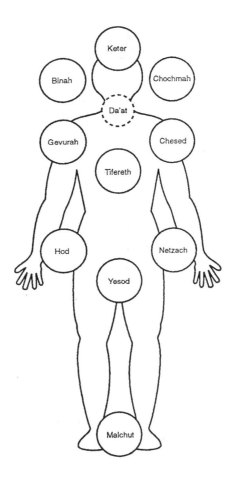

The Continuing Journey

There is another model for journey to God, for alignment of the *sefirot,* that was born out of evolving human consciousness, and the bubbling up of new God-energy.

The linear, hierarchical, top to bottom, authoritarian structure is replaced by a circular, web-like structure.

The *sefirot* are in an egalitarian circle, where each *sefirah* spins, whirls, and tumbles in on itself.

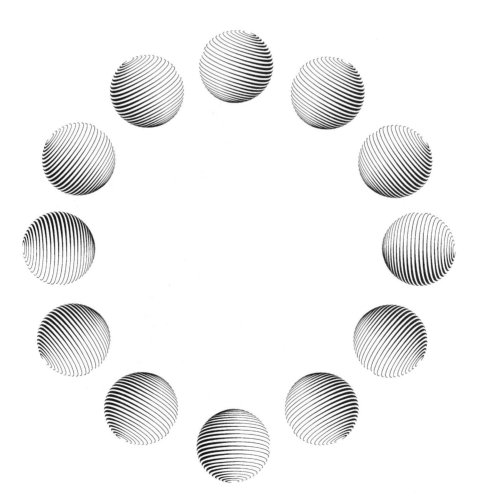

At the same time, the *sefirot* are in constant motion, spinning, whirling, and tumbling in on each other, constantly changing place, interweaving with each other.

In this image, the way to God is not to climb up a ladder to reach up to God, but, rather, to be in constantly moving, interwoven inter-action with God, to be—in the words of the poet Walt Whitman—"like two waves rolling over each other and inter-wetting each other."

This image is a "snapshot in time," meaning that in another nano-second, the configuration, which is in constant motion, will be totally different.

Whether or not they were consciously aware of it, this model was embraced by the 18th century Chasidim, who rejected the notion that there is any hierarchy of people or ideas on the journey to God. While they were non-egalitarian concerning women's rights and roles in Jewish life, the Chasidim championed egalitarianism in regard to equal access to God. There can be, they insisted, no secret avenue open only to the elite; there can be no test of scholarship or learning. The approach to God cannot be hidden or veiled. Each person has complete, unfettered access to God through (choose one or more): personal piety, text-learning, stories and parables, ritual observance, deep meditation, and fervent, joyful prayer, chant, and dance.

Together the Kabbalistic and Chasidic approaches to God inform many of the patterns of modern prayer. Yet, still, the modern age suggests one more Kabbalistic model.

THE NEW TREE OF LIFE

◆

We are surely in the midst of an Axial Age—a massive, sweeping shift in the world-order. The old, venerable institutions of life—government, finance, communications, education, medicine, religion—are experiencing great challenge and undergoing great change. As familiar structures are taken apart, much is in chaos and confusion.

Our spiritual lives reflect the upheaval that is taking place both in our world and in our religious institutions and practices, and, for many, the way to God has become blurred.

Some have turned back to the old, gentle religious beliefs, traditions, and practices that are well known, and that bring comfort.

Some have become rigid fundamentalists, holding on for dear existence to the forms and the touchstones of the past; resolutely opposing even one iota of change; insisting that their way is the only way.

Some have gone searching for God in new, or renewed places. Some have embraced a widely defined "spirituality." Some have turned to the age-old Spirit-based kinships and their spiritual guides and teachers to immerse in ancient wisdom. Some have chosen the life of quiet, sometimes isolated, contemplation and meditation.

Some have made "new gods" of materialism, or hedonism, or secularism, or humanism, or any of the other "isms" that promise personal ego-gratification, yet can lead to alienation, existential loneliness, and communal diffusion.

We are surely part of a paramount unfolding shift in the interrelationship between God, humankind, and the universe.

Like every other religion and faith community, Judaism is in the throes of radical—some would say "revolutionary"—change.

Judaism's first 2,000 years—approximately 1800 BCE, until the beginning of the Common Era—is called the "Biblical Period," or "Biblical Judaism." This era was characterized by the establishment and the development of the covenant between God and the Jewish people, and, at the very same time, by the ever-present possibility of individual prophecy—the notion that God could and would reveal Divine will to any person at any time.

At the beginning of the Common Era, some 2,000 years ago, Biblical Judaism began to give way to Judaism's second era, the time we now call "The Rabbinic Period," or "Rabbinic Judaism." The rabbis and sages effectively cut off individual prophecy by teaching that God's continuing revelation came only through them, that they, alone, would receive and transmit God's word (and record it, for the generations, in the *Mishnah,* the *Talmud,* and later law literature.) This scholar-centered and law-based religion is practiced as "mainline" Judaism to this very day.

Judaism's age-old ethical laws are still widely accepted and embraced, and remain a profound influence. Yet, today, only in the Orthodox world, is fully-observed Jewish ritual law the norm. In the liberal Jewish world, most people consider ritual law informative, instructive, and, perhaps, inspirational, but not binding. Most contemporary Jews largely ignore and little practice the many facets of Jewish ritual law.

So, slowly yet profoundly, Rabbinic Judaism is giving over to Judaism's third era—a time where following the details of the ritual law is no longer the primary means of the Jewish relationship to God.

This new era is characterized by a deep commitment to the communal covenant, to creating and being part of sacred community. Yet, at the same time, its primacy is the return to the very real notion that each person—each individual human soul—can have a deep, personal, intimate relationship with God; to talk directly with God, and to hear directly from God.*

At its core, this new era is based in the personal, ever-real, ever-living personal covenant between each person—each soul—and God.

And, so, we seek a new Kabbalistic model for our day that is rooted in the authenticity of the ages; that reflects the evolving consciousness and new God-energy of our time; that weaves together the guideposts of both the linear and the circular. And, most, we seek a model that affirms and celebrates the relationship between each person and God, and that gives us a wise, wondrous, and very practical way to connect and communicate with God.

The Kabbalistic model for our age modifies the random chance swirling motion of the *sefirot* in the circular model by restoring the image of the linear Tree of Life. It changes the order in which we engage the *sefirot*, so that **the new image of the journey to God is a spiral.**

In this spiral, there is a sense of numbered order, as we move from *sefirah* #1 through the *sefirot* until we reach *sefirah* #12, with each *sefirah* taking on new order, new meaning, and new purpose for the journey.

Yet, even in order, in the spiral, there is constant movement, constant connection, constant interaction.

The spiral is like the Kabbalah's name for God—*Ein Sof*. It is infinite—without beginning and without end; always and forever.

---

*For a full explanation of this new phenomenon, please see Reb Wayne's book, *Dancing With God: Everyday Steps to Jewish Spiritual Renewal,* (HarperSan Francisco) which, in its paperback edition is now called, *Soul Judaism: Dancing with God into a New Era.* (Jewish Lights.)

This spiral configuration comes to us with echoes from the deep past.

The ancients were enjoined to wear fringes on the corners of their garments as a physical sign of God's loving commandments—an observance that many Jews still follow today, and which manifests in the ritual prayer garb, the *tallit*. The strings of the fringes are made into knots and swirls to symbolically represent the number 613—the number of *mitzvot*-commandments in the Torah. Antiquity's string, spiraling around itself, representing the word of God, is today's renewed image of our interconnection with the Divine.

And, the spiral configuration comes to us in the most recent scientific discoveries of the mysteries of the universe.

Modern physics teaches the "string theory"—that, rather than zero-dimensional particles, the single, fundamental building blocks of the universe are multi-dimensional vibrating, spinning, swirling, spiraling strings. Some proponents of the string theory teach that it leads to the conclusion that the universe is 26-dimensional. How interesting! For, the *gematria* (the numerical value of the Hebrew letters) of the biblical name of God, יהוה *yud, hey, vav, hey,* pronounced *Yahweh,* or, alternately, *Adonai,* is 26! Modern science's new cosmology is imaged in the Kabbalistic model of a spiraling string, that lives in dimensions spelling the name of God!

At the same time, science is mapping the human genome, the double-stranded, spiraling DNA, which holds keys to the questions of human existence. And, some say that DNA is currently expanding and growing, and will eventually be twelve interconnected, swirling spiraled strands.

Science does not invent or create anew; it discovers and records what is already there. All that modern science is now beginning to understand is a reflection of the Kabbalistic model that has now bubbled up from antiquity—the ever-spiraling relationship between God, humankind, and the universe.

As physicist Dr. Robert Jastrow, the former head of NASA, puts it, ". . . the scientist has lived by the power of reason, he has scaled the mountains of ignorance, and is about to conquer the highest peak. As he pulls himself over the final rock, he is greeted by a band of theologians who have been sitting there for centuries."

The new order, enhanced meaning, and purpose of each *sefirah* for this SoulJourney to God is:

1. **TIFERET. The Heart Space.**
   Coming Into God's Holy Presence

2. **GEVURAH. The Place of Ingathering & Boundaries.**
   Coming Into God's Protection

3. **CHESED. Unconditional Love.**
   Feeling God's Love

4. **NETZACH. The Place of Outward Creative Energy.**
   Toning the Vibration of God's Love

5. **HOD. The Place of Inner Creative Energy.**
   Becoming One with the Breath of God.

6. **BINAH. The Place of Direct, Felt-Sense Experience.**
   Being God's Co-Creative Partner

7. **CHOCHMAH. The Place of Conscious Intelligence.**
   Co-Creating God's Worlds

8. **YESOD. The Life Force.**
   Manifesting God's Design

9. **THE BACK OF DA'AT. The Entrance into God's Time Tunnel, at the High Heart.**
   Coming Into Perfect Alignment with God

10. **MALCHUT / SHECHINAH. Manifest Materiality.**
    Being in Oneness with God

11. **KETER. The Dwelling Place of God & The Union With God.**
    Communicating with God

12. **THE FRONT OF DA'AT. The Emerging from God's Time Tunnel with New-Found Truth, at the High Heart.**
    Ever-Experiencing God and GodSelf

Can we picture this spiral?

Can we even begin to imagine it?

It is certainly multi-dimensional, intersecting many worlds at the same time. It surely is in constant motion, whirling, swirling, and twirling like its circular predecessor; turning inside and outside of itself. All the while, with the grace of delicate, elegant dance, it holds its shape and the particular positions of each *sefirah* within the configuration. It is, perhaps, rainbow colored, sparkling and glittering in its dazzling beauty.

With our three dimensional eyes, the best we can sense is the image of a hologram, which has unlimited depth, boundless space, and unending motion.

Like the Kabbalisitc notion of the Infinite God, from and to whom our spiritual journey spirals, the spiral Tree of Life is itself *Ein Sof*, without beginning and without end.

The Spiral Tree of Life image looks like this:

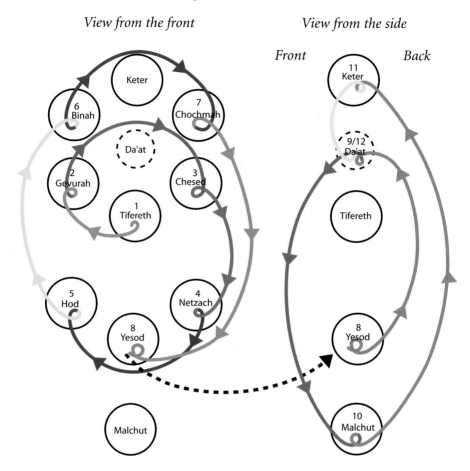

View from the front

View from the side

The colors that connect the *sefirot* are the same colors that are generally associated with the Hindu concept (all wisdom is universal!) of *chakras*, the centers of spiritual power located in the body.

In your spiraling, you begin the spiral to God in *Tifereth, the Heart Space.*

The color BLUE, associated with truth, takes you to *Gevurah.*

PINK, associated with the energy of love, takes you to *Chesed.*

GREEN, associated with life and healing, takes you to *Netzach.*

RED, associated with groundedness, takes you to *Hod.*

YELLOW, associated with the energy of power, takes you to *Binah.*

PURPLE, associated with the energy of Divine connection, takes you to *Chochmah.*

ORANGE, associated with creative, sexual energy, takes you to *Yesod.*

Now, the spiral, which has been moving up and down, begins to move from front to back.

GOLD, associated with the Divine Masculine, takes you to the Back of *Da'at.*

COPPER and SILVER which take you to *Malchut* and then to *Keter,* are associated with the *Shechinah,* the Divine Feminine.

PLATINUM, which takes you to the Front of *Da'at,* is associated with the Full Source, the fully braided and united Divine Feminine and Divine Masculine.

Using this spiral configuration of the Tree of Life to journey to God will result in a change to the long-established fixed order of prayer, and will introduce some new prayers (all sourced in biblical and Jewish liturgical texts) sung and chanted to some new (but old) melodies.

It is understandable that there will be those who resist change to the well-established, well-known, and comfortable. Yet, remember: for now, the old order of the public communal worship services remains the same (although it, too, begs for revision.)

This new order is for private, individual prayers that bring each and every person—you!—into personal, intimate relationship with God.

This new order brings you to God more swiftly and more intensely. That is its wondrous excitement, and its invaluable worth and merit.

We are not 13th or 16th century Kabbalists. Nor are we 18th century Chasidim. We are not scholars or historians of Kabbalah; nor are we deeply immersed in day and night study or mystic practice. Yet, like the Kabbalists, we want to come to God through deep, sweet, powerful meditation, and, like the Chasidim, we want to come to God through ecstatically joyful prayer.

We are the egalitarian neo-Kabbalists, the new Kabbalists, and the egalitarian neo-Chasidism, the new Chasidim, who offer a new model that honors and celebrates the teachings and the patterns of the past, and, at the very same time, creates a new form, to weave a new, mystical pathway to being with God.

Spiraling To God

The God we seek is not an old man with a long white beard, sitting on a Heavenly throne.

The God we seek is not a Santa Claus, who automatically and without discernment, gives us anything we ask.

The God we seek is the Infinite, Ever-Present, Eternal, All-Encompassing; the Everything of the Everything.

God is the Wholeness, the Totality, the Oneness of the universe—male and female, light and dark and shadow, us and other, justice and compassion, pain and comfort, good and evil, life, and death, and life eternal. There is nothing in the universe that is not God. God is the Source and Substance of All.

This is God who made us, and who knows us, and who cares about us; who watches over us and protects us; who weeps with us in our pain, lifts us up from the depths, and comforts us in our sorrow; who empowers our strengths, heralds our triumphs, and celebrates our joys.

This is God who loves us.

Now, here comes the part that is sometimes hard to understand.

If God is Everything, and since I, and an elephant, and a chair, are part of Everything, then I—and the elephant and the chair—am God. Right?

Some—especially in this new age—would say, "That is exactly right. You are God."

But the Kabbalists would say, "Not quite." We do not claim an un-differentiated Oneness with God. Yes, God is Everywhere. God is *in* the elephant. The elephant is *of* God. God is *in* the chair. The chair is *of* God. God is *in* me. I am *of* God. My breath is the Breath of God; my spirit is the Spirit of God. God is Within me. But I am not God.

As the great modern spiritual guide, Rabbi Dr. Abraham Joshua Heschel *zt"l* taught, we do not want to be the mystic who seeks to become one with God. We do not want to be the ecstatic who seeks to separate mind from body in finding God. We do not want to be the psychotic who goes mad in the quest. We do not even want to be the poet, lest we confuse our intent with God's intent, our will with God's will.

Rather, we want to be what Heschel taught that we all can be—the prophet, who can find God, know God, be in relationship with God, be sourced by God, talk to God, hear God's word and will, and be God's messenger on Earth.

I want to know God and be with God from "the insides of the insides." I want God to be at the very center of my being.

And God needs and wants all of us to be part of the Divine, to be wholly of God. God wants us to be in the "inside of the insides," to reside at the Heart of all Being. You and I are Within God. We are at the very center of God's Being.

So, in Kabbalah, we seek the most intimate union with God.

I seek to merge my Self with God's Self, my being with God's Being. I want to come into alignment, attunement, at-One-ment with God. I want to be in the deepest spiritual intention, the highest spiritual connection, the highest and the deepest human consciousness. I want to be wholly present in God's design and flow, in God's "energy field," God's "light-sphere," God's "wavelength," I want to be a conduit to God and a channel of God.

When we come to the *sefirah* in the spiral where we talk directly with God— the 11th *sefirah*, Keter, which is the place where matter and spirit meet, the place of union with God, the place where we say "*Hineini.* Here I Am"—we will consider the attitudes and expectations, the needs and the desires, that both God and we have in the encounter. Yet, that is only a matter of form—vital, but form, nevertheless—not substance.

Let there be no doubt; let there be no question.

I can be with God.

You can be with God.

This Kabbalistic-Chasidic spiritual practice has roots in antiquity and enchantingly renews the tradition in this moment. It is deeply Jewish, using authentic Jewish language, rhythms, melodies, and chants. And, it can be embraced by everyone.

In this spiral-*sefirot*-journey, the collective "We" of most Jewish prayer is replaced by the first person singular, "I." This spiritual practice is individual; it is personal; it is intimate. It is you and God—alone, together.

The prayers and chants of Kabbalah's new spiral-*sefirot* Tree of Life are laser-focused to traverse time and space in order to bring you to God very quickly. You can be with God in God-time. "A thousand years in Your sight, O God, are like yesterday. The days of our lives are like a fleeting shadow." (Ps. 90:4; 102:12)

Your meditative conversation with God can be concentrated, intense and profound, all the while being sweet, gentle, and loving.

All it takes is twenty minutes a day.

20 Minutes With God

You can adopt this life-changing Kabbalistic practice by following the simple instructions in this book, and by learning the simple chants that are on the audio CD that comes with the book.

Even if 20 MINUTE KABBALAH seems a bit intimidating at first, or if you feel that it is "beyond you," that the concepts are too hard or that the melodies are too difficult, you will soon come to know that it is really very light, and sweet, and lovely—and it will enthrall your soul and "take hold" in your being.

So, just begin.

Begin prayer by praying. Think that you don't know how, that you might not have the proper spiritual intent? Then follow the guidance of the Chassidic rebbe who said, "I pray that I will be able to pray."

Don't know what to say? Use these 20 MINUTE KABBALAH chants. They throw open the Gates.

Still unsure that you can do it? Then, in the words of the prayer recited by traditional Jews three times a day, everyday, ask God to help you speak to God: "O, God, open my lips so that my mouth can declare praise of You." Explicitly, in the words of Rabbi Sheldon Zimmerman, ask God to, "Please listen to my call; help me find the words, help me find the strength within, help me shape my mouth, my voice, my heart, so that I can direct my spirit to You in prayer."

The way to faith is through faith; the way to faith is through doing faith. As the Children of Israel responded in the desert when they received Torah, "We will do it, and then we will come to understand it." (Ex. 24:7)

Do faith, and you will come to embrace faith.

Wherever your place in the realm of God, spirit, prayer, meditation, and mysticism, this 20 MINUTE KABBALAH practice is for you.

The spiral-*sefirot*-journey will take you higher and higher and deeper and deeper, right into the "inside of the insides." Your mind, your heart, your soul—your entire being—will connect with God. And, then, in the most intimate, soul-satisfying, heart-filling way, you can talk to God, and listen as God talks to you.

20 Minute Kabbalah:
How It Works

- **There are twelve spiral-*sefirot*-prayers corresponding
  to the twelve *sefirot*.** Each prayer has perfect place in the
  spiral, and deep meaning and purpose for its own *sefirah*.
The explanation given with each *sefirah* will illuminate that *sefirah* for you,
and make clear how each prayer is connected to its *sefirah*.

- **Each *sefirah*-prayer is addressed to God**—the God with
  whom you are coming to be in intimate connection
  and conversation.
The most well-known and popular Name of God is the biblical name
יהוה the Hebrew letters *yud, hey, vav, hey,* pronounced *Yahweh.* This
name implies the Being-ness of God—God was, God is, God will always be. In traditional Jewish practice, the name *Yahweh* is considered
too holy to be spoken—even in Scripture reading or prayer. So, the
substitute name for God that is most often used in speaking text and
prayer is *Adonai,* which means "Master."

In all the *sefirah*-prayer-chants given here, we use the name
Adonai for God. Yet, we recognize that some are uncomfortable with
the word *Adonai,* because it holds strong masculine, hierarchical, authoritarian energy.

There are scores of names of God; each carrries its own designation, purpose, and energy. Here, we offer three alternative names to call God.

One is **Shechinah,** the name that holds the feminine, in-dwelling, nurturing, web-weaving energy.

Another is **HaShem,** which means "The Name." This is a genderless name for God, which eliminates any discomfort with addressing God's masculine or feminine energy, and, instead is all inclusive of all of God's energies and attributes.

Finally, we offer **Anochi,** which means "I" as a name to address God. *Anochi* is also genderless, all inclusive, and implies "I, Myself; the Wholeness of my being; the Me-ness of Me." *Anochi* is, at the same time, both the transcendent God, and the immanent God—the God Within.

In your *sefirah*-prayers, call God whatever name makes God most known to you, the name that makes God most accessible to you, the name that is most comfortable for you. On any given day—or, even for any given *sefirah*-prayer on the same day—you can switch or alternate. God does not care by what Name you call. God will answer to every Name and any Name. Just call, and God will respond.

The *sefirah*-prayer-chants on the audio CD first call God *Adonai,* and, then, offer a short example of calling God *Shechinah, HaShem,* and *Anochi.*

- **Each sefirah-prayer has its own chant;** the music of each
  chant is specifically selected for the vibrational connection
  that enhances the *sefirah's* place and purpose in the spiral.

You may recognize the texts of many of the *sefirah*-prayers, because they are well-known, core parts of traditional Jewish worship services. Other prayers—all from some place in scripture or liturgy—are paired with a particular *sefirah,* to partner the energy of the *sefirah* with the corresponding energy of a particular melody.

You may also recognize the melodies of some of these chants. They are adapted to the words of these prayers from well-known liturgical and scriptural chant-melodies. They are deeply embedded in the collective Jewish psyche, for they hold ancient, deep, and very powerful prayer energy and vibration. Your soul will recognize and remember them, and rejoice in their sound.

- **One of the beauties of 20 MINUTE KABBALAH is that this daily spiritual practice can be done in the manner that is most comfortable for you**—sitting or standing, eyes opened or closed.

If you choose a particular time and place for your practice, you may wish to wear one or more pieces of the traditional Jewish "prayer-uniform." A covered head is a sign of respect and honor for God. Wrapping in the fringed prayer shawl, the *tallit,* is like wrapping in a prayer-blanket of intimacy with God. The arm and head *tephillin* acknowledge your connection to God through heart and third eye.

Yet, you do not have to be anywhere special or wear anything special, because your chants and meditations can be done anytime and anywhere.

While at first, it is probably best to set a regular time and place for your practice, once you have learned and memorized the order and the meanings of the *sefirot,* and the chant that accompanies each, you can come to God anywhere—in the morning shower, on the drive or on the train to work, walking on the street, sitting on a park bench, at work, at school, in your office or on your assembly line, at lunch, during a coffee-break, on the drive back home, walking the dog, at the gym or on the treadmill, sitting on the couch or in the backyard, standing at the kitchen stove, on an airplane, at the beach, on the golf course, or swimming laps.

Anywhere. Everywhere.

1. **Begin your daily journey with the Energy Balance.** These deep breaths balance your energy with the Earth's; put you

in touch with the breath of God within you; and open
your being as a clear, pure channel of the Divine.

2. **Then, recite the prayer for Standing at The Burning Bush.**
This little prayer aligns the limited Self with the unlimited
Soul, and calls forth your full being to stand with God.

3. **Then, chant the verse for Coming Into The World of Spirit.**
Take its words into the quiet place of your being.

4. **Focus on the name and the meaning of the first *sefirah*
in the spiral — *Tiferet*.** For the first few weeks, you will
probably want to read the explanation given here in the
book. Over time, you will know and feel the meaning of
each *sefirah* and its prayer, and your heart and soul will
instinctively take you there.

5. **Chant or recite the prayer of the *sefirah*.** Your chanting of
this prayer can take 60 to 90 seconds. You will be amazed
at how deep and how high your prayer can go in well less
than two minutes.

**Using the Hebrew or the transliterations into English, and by
listening to the audio CD, you can learn to chant the Hebrew of the
spiral-*sefirot*-prayers.**

If you do not know Hebrew, you can learn a little bit. Why not? We
have all learned some Hindu, and Buddhist, and Native American, and
Christian, and Muslim words, and, songs, and chants. They live in our
collective souls, where all is One. Hebrew — the ancient language of
creation, covenant, and ultimate redemption — will touch you at the
deepest primordial place in your being.

There are five chants in this spiritual practice that each have only
one Hebrew word. Because of their great vibrational power, we hope
that you will consider chanting at least these five words in Hebrew.

Yet, if you are more comfortable, chant the English translations.

Or—if it deepens your practice (as it does ours)—chant both Hebrew and English.

Or, chant wordless melodies—called *niggunim*—because the very sounds carry the power of the words.

Or, if you are not comfortable with chanting, you can recite the words.

Or, if you are not comfortable with speaking the words aloud, you can say them in your mind's-heart.

Or, you can stare at them on the page, because even in their written form, the words—their letters and white spaces between the letters—carry their own vibrational energy that spirals with God.

The chants are given on the audio CD in a quiet, contemplative, meditative mode. Yet, depending on your mood at any given moment, you can quicken the rhythm and the tempo to make many of the chants more vibrant, more pulsating, and more joyous.

Your needs and feelings will set the tone of each of your prayers and your God talk.

A word about chanting each prayer: "Attention must be paid." You want to know well the meaning of the words you say—their place in the tradition and their purpose in your spiral journey. You do not want your recitation to be without understanding, or to be empty, or, worse, to become rote and without meaning.

And, you want to know these prayers, because there is great inherent energy in each of them—an energy which suffuses this whole spiritual practice. Each word swirls, and vibrates, and spirals with its own animated vitality and power.

At the same time, the chant can become repetitive, and, now and then, you can get caught up in the melody alone, and stop paying attention to the meaning of the words. And that, too, is fine, for that is what chant is designed to do. "Getting lost" in the chant, and in the empty space of the void, is a different form of "paying attention." You go deeper and deeper into your soul, to that unconscious place from where new thought and new understanding arises. Chant draws you into the emptiness, and you emerge renewed.

One more word about chant that comes to us from Rabbi Shefa Gold, this generation's most compelling chant leader. "The most powerful moment of the chant happens in the silence that follows."

These chant-melodies will "stick in your head," and it will not be long before you find yourself humming or chanting one or more of the melodies at various times and places throughout the day—unconsciously extending your 20 minute spiritual practice into all the spaces in your life.

The audio CD has two parts.

In the first part, the chants are slowly taught, one by one,

so that you can learn the words and the melodies,

and so that you can choose the Name(s)

by which you want to call God.

In the second part of the CD, the chants are sung

without interuption

—in Hebrew, then English, then Hebrew again—

so that you can establish your daily practice

by singing along.

To obtain additional copies of

the 20 MINUTE KABBALAH CHANTS AUDIO CD

by download or on a disk,

please visit the website

www.20MinuteKabbalah.com

---

6. **When you have finished the prayer-chant of the first *sefirah*, breathe deeply two or three times** to fix and set the prayer in the Four Worlds of your being.

7. **Then, in order, go on to the next *sefirah*, and then each succeeding *sefirah***—focusing on the name and the meaning of the *sefirah*, chanting the prayer, and breathing deeply after each one.

8. **When you come to the 11th *sefirah*, *Keter*, this is the place for your meditation / conversation / communication with God.** You present yourself to God with the chant הִנֵּנִי *Hineini* "Here I Am." You are in the "I Am" Holy Presence of God, with your "I Am" GodSelf.

Some suggestions for your mindset, heartset, and soulset for being in the Holy Presence are offered in the section on *Keter* later in this book.

9. **As you begin to leave the Holy Presence,** breathe deeply, and chant the *sefirah*-prayer for *sefirah* #12—The Front of *Da'at*. Then, breathe deeply.

10. **Then, recite the process for Remembering.** Once you are ready to immerse in the everyday activities of life, the twenty minute practice of chant and meditation can quickly fade. But, you want to remember. You want to hold on to the thoughts and the feelings from your spiral-*sefirah*-journey for longer and longer. You want them to permeate your being, and to become more and more part of you; to be like rich musical notes that are held and sustained, and continue to sweeten your whole existence. And, tomorrow, you want to build on today's journey, on today's conversation with God.

    So, following the prayers and chants of the complete spiral-*sefirot*-journey, there is a little process to recite to help you to remember. It only takes a few seconds to say, but it holds great power in your soul.

11. **Then, if it applies, recite the *Kaddish* for Celebrating Souls in the Light,** or, if you choose, a different prayer of praise—"The Lord's Prayer."

12. **Complete your daily practice with the Seal, chanting "Shalom."**

13. **Then breathe deeply,** and begin to come back into this physical world from your spiritual meditative state.

    It is delicious to be in deep conversation with God; it feels good to be in Sacred Space, bathed in God's Light. You probably would rather stay there than come back to this physical world with all its vicissitudes. But it can be spiritually and physically draining to stay in the Light for too long. So, make your journey back to this world slowly and carefully—but, assuredly.

14. **At whatever times it feels right and good to you, recite the affirmations in "Sky Blue: Above and Below."**

These are powerful—and sweet—statements that anchor in what you and God have done together on the particular day, and speak your intention to be an integral part of the unfolding process of transformation and perfection for our world.

15. **Then, be kind to yourSelf.** Take good care of yourSelf.

16. **Remember Beyond Today.** We invite you to keep a daily diary or journal to record your feelings, thoughts, and impressions about your experiences. By journaling— today's "fancy" word for making a few notes to yourself about yourself, your activities, and your state of being— you keep the record of your journey to God and your unfolding relationship with God.

Some people have titled their journal their "BOOK OF GOD."

Just before you begin your daily 20 MINUTE KABBALAH practice for the very first time, you might want to begin your "BOOK OF GOD" with a little note to God.

"Dear God, I've always wanted to ask You . . ."

Do not think too long nor too deeply; just let your heart and your soul pour out your questions to God.

Then write, "Dear God, These are the desires of my heart. . . . ."

Again, with free-flowing stream of consciousness—and your unconscious that will emerge—express your longings and your yearnings.

As part of your daily practice, each day—or whenever it feels right—write a few sentences about your experience and your feelings in coming to God.

Near the end of this book, as EndPiece II, we offer you some suggested questions to consider about each *sefirah*-prayer.

These questions are only guidelines to stimulate your thinking; what you write in your "BOOK OF GOD" will be the outpouring of your own heart and soul.

Every two or three weeks, repeat your initial two notes to God— Dear God, I've always wanted to ask You. . . ." and "Dear God, These are the desires of my heart. . . ."

Every once in a while, go back into your "BOOK OF GOD" and read what you have previously written—especially in your "Dear God" notes.

We think that you will be amazed and very, very pleased to see how your 20 MINUTE KABBALAH practice grows and enhances your life, and how your relationship with God becomes so deep and so sweet.

Just like the sacred scripture of our ancestors, in your "BOOK OF GOD," you are recording your encounters with God. You are writing a holy book.

Always

As you spiral with God everyday, your prayers will become richer; your meditations will become deeper; your relationship with God will become fuller.

You just have to resolve that you will always come to God.

Even with the ease that a twenty minute spiritual practice offers, the challenge is to keep doing it.

Beginning with enthusiasm is simple. Continuing each and every day can be hard. All the normal challenges of life can get in the way. You oversleep. The baby is sick. The deadline at work looms. You forgot to pack the school lunches. Your busy life threatens to overwhelm, and even twenty minutes carved out of your day sometimes seems like a luxury.

Or, sometimes, even with the best of spiritual intent, the twenty minute practice does not seem to be working for you. Today, tomorrow, the next day, you are in deep spiritual connection with God. But the day after, and the day after that, and all next week, you somehow miss the connection, and God seems far away. Perhaps you are distracted; perhaps you have too many other things on your mind; perhaps you are tired or not feeling well.

Or, perhaps you are angry with God, and you are "not speaking" with God right now.

Long ago, our sages knew this problem. They hoped that every person would feel and experience the spiritual intent—which they called *kavannah*—everyday. But, they were realists; they knew that many things can come between us and our intentions. So they set up the ordered, fixed structure of prayer—which they called *keva*—to keep us in connection, even when we feel disconnected; to give us something to say, even when we do not have our own words. They intuited that if we "don't feel like it" for long enough, we will stop trying. But, if we always have something to do and say with God, and if we keep doing and saying it, even when we don't want to, then, eventually, from out of our constant doing, the real intent will reemerge.

The sages taught: From out of *keva* will come *kavannah*. A modern writer put it this way: "Out of repetition, sometimes magic is forced to rise."

Or, simply put by the contemporary advertisement: "Just do it." Always.

On the Journey

"Where," the great sage was asked, "is God?"
"God is everywhere you let God in."

By coming to God in daily Kabbalistic meditation, by crossing the seeming abyss and coming to know that there is no distance to the Infinite Oneness, you can come into union, into being-ness with God.

You are in intimate connection. You are filled to overflowing with God-energy. You speak the yearnings of your heart and soul. You feel so loved. Oh, how you feel loved!

You come to know the transcendent God, the God who creates, and commands, and sustains—the God of history and of destiny.

And you come to know the immanent God, the God Within.

Your wonderings can be sated; your questions can have response, for you merge with universal, eternal knowledge; you intuitively feel-sense the innermost secrets of the universe.

As your relationship with God ripens and grows, as with any other intimate relationship, there will be times of burden and times of glory; times of great joy and times of bitter disappointment; times of bewilderment and times of certainty. Ask for grace and dignity, wisdom and gratitude. And they will be given.

As you are bathed in God's Light, like Moses, you become a mirror reflection of the Light of the Divine.

Here on Earth, you can become a God-like co-creator who feeds the hungry; clothes the naked, educates the illiterate, cares for the widow; tells the truth, gives fair weights and measures, pays a day laborer at the end of the day. You can reflect God as you honor your parents, are kind to the stranger, "do not put a stumbling block before the blind," work for justice and peace, and love your neighbor as you love yourSelf.

"In Your light, O God, do we see Light." (Ps. 36:10)

You are, in the image of the contemporary mystic, Rabbi David Cooper, "God-ing." The sparks of the Divine inspirit and enflame you, and open you to the infinite possibilities of life and living.

You are in your "God-ness."
You are with God, and God is with you.
You are within God, and God is within you.
Heaven and Earth touch.
It is Eden once again.
The spiral spirals.
From God. To God.
To God. From God.
The spiral spirals.
God is here.
Your soul is here.
The moment is here.
The Gates are always open.
The Bush always burns.
The spiral spirals.
Without Beginning. Without End.
The spiral spirals.
Come.
Enter the spiral.
Be the spiral.
EveryThing, EveryWhere, EveryOne, awaits.

20 Minute Kabbalah: The Daily Spiritual Practice

◆

Hello, God

Worship, prayer, is far more than the recitation of words from a book, much more than an intellectual exercise of approaching God with rational thoughts and reasoned arguments.

To really pray is to *daven* (a Yiddish word that comes either from the Latin for "Divine," or from the Lithuanian for "gift.") To *daven* is to come to God with an open heart and soul, with the depths of emotional celebration or need, with soul cries of anguish or joy, with the deepest of desire to touch the Divine.

To *daven* means to truly connect with God; to be completely engaged in the experience; to be wholly affected by the words, the music, the mood, the encounter; to be caught up in the immediate and absolute reality of speaking to God; to be in full and deep conversation with God. To *daven* means to be certain that God is listening; and to hear God in response.

Davennen (daven-ing) is like being in love. It can be defined and described with words, but never fully explained, because it is of the heart and soul. Like love, *davennen* is experienced and deeply felt in its sublime connection, its profound power, and its spiritual potency. It is being fully caught up in the intense, awesome, life-affirming energy of being with your lover, God.

We invite you to *daven* the Tree of Life.

We invite you to be in love with God.

ENERGY BALANCE

To enter into Sacred Space, and the Spiral-*Sefirot*-Prayers, it is helpful to balance your body, mind, emotional, and spiritual energies with the Earth's Energy.

Follow these steps to do the ENERGY BALANCE.

Either standing or sitting (whichever is more comfortable for you):

1. Plant your feet firmly on the ground.

2. Breathe deeply, inhaling and exhaling three times.

3. Cross your arms over your chest, hands at your shoulders.

   Breathe deeply three times.

4. Reverse the cross.

   Breathe deeply three times.

5. Put your hands in your lap (or at your sides, if you are standing.)

   Breathe deeply three times.

STANDING AT THE BURNING BUSH

To begin your journey into the Holy Presence, recite this prayer to align the limited self with the unlimited Soul; to call forth your full being to stand with God.

The Bush burns.
The Gates are open.
I am here.

Source of all Worlds,
Breath of all Life,
Oneness of all Being:
I open my heart to Your Holy Presence.
I open my soul to Your Enveloping Voice.

Be with me.
Embrace me.
Hear me.

Answer me.
Please, answer me,
on this day when I call.

Guide me.
Challenge me.
Inspirit me.
Bless me.

Hold me in Your great compassion,
and keep me in Your saving truth.

—*brought down by ELKD & WD*

COMING INTO THE WORLD OF SPIRIT

Standing at the bush, ready to enter the Spiral Tree of Life, focus your thoughts and your spiritual intentions on God.

Breathe deeply three times and, then, chant:

הרפו ודעו כי אנכי אלהים

Har-fu u'd'u ki Anochi Elohim

Be still and know that I Am God.

—*Ps. 46:11*

Breathe deeply three more times, and quiet your mind; open your heart and your soul to God's Being—and yours.

In a soft whisper, recite this stanza three times, and let the meaning of the words fill you, and echo in you.

Be still and know that I Am God.

Be still and know that I Am.

Be still.

Be.

1.

Tiferet—Beauty

The Heart Space
balance / the portal to all other dimensions

Coming Into God's Holy Presence

Before beginning any strenuous physical activity, or participating in an athletic event—chopping wood, playing tennis, taking a long hike, or, surely, running a marathon—most people "warm-up" by stretching, exercising, perhaps jogging a short distance.

Traditionally, it has been the same for the "spiritual marathon" of coming to God. You need to get ready, to "warm-up" your heart and soul. After just getting out of bed in the morning, or during the afternoon of a busy day, or at the end of a tiring, perhaps, stress-filled day, it is hard to just plunge into direct conversation with God. You need a few moments to move from the material world into the world of spirit; you need a little time to get into the mood for your encounter. That is why the traditional order of the Jewish worship service begins with introductory, "warm-up" prayers of thanksgiving and praise to God.

Then, when the time comes, the communal prayer leader calls out *Bar'chu*, "Come let us praise God, to whom all praise is due." The worshippers—by now "warmed-up"—respond, "Yes. We are ready." "Let us praise God, to whom all praise is due, forever and ever."

The new Kabbalistic model, the new order of prayer, reflects the reality that the full immanent God is always present and available; and it is only your limited consciousness that prevents you from being aware of God's presence. All it takes to find God is for you to make the choice to open the fullness of your being, to simply look and discover that God is with you all the time—ready and waiting for connection.

The psalmist sings, "Open the Gates. . . ." The reality is that the Gates are always open. The Bush always burns.

Each and every one of us lives with God in the Heart Space of the *sefirah Tiferet*. So, just as God is always ready to be with you, you are always ready to be with God. "It is not too hard, neither is it far off. . . . It is not in Heaven . . . neither is it beyond the sea. . . . It is close to you, in your mouth and in your heart." (after Deut. 30: 12-14) God is just waiting for you to call. Nothing is in your way; the vagaries of life are but minor distraction.

You are already in the Heart place. You are eager and anxious; you can be with God swiftly and without delay. Your spirit does not require any "warm-up." All you need do is turn and face God.

And so, from the Heart's full and open presence—from *Tiferet*—you begin connecting to God.

Rather than using the communal call to worship, you use a personal call to worship, the words of Psalm 16:8, "I place God before me always."

Unlike the usual formula of Jewish prayer which is recited in the collective—we—this prayer is individual: "*I* place God before *me* . . ." Me. You are saying: This is a connection, a conversation, between God and me—no one else, just the two of us. This is coming to God, being with God in the most intimate, personal way.

What does it mean to "place God before me"? It certainly does not require having an anthropomorphic picture of God. You do not have to see God in any image or form. In the current vernacular, it means to "put God in my face"—to be fully conscious and aware of the Divine presence, to be in God energy, in the Divine design, in God's flow.

And, if you place God always before you, then, God is between you and whatever happens, whatever the situation or circumstance, whatever the tragedy or the triumph of your life. Before anything and everything else, first, you see God. And, in seeing God, you see your Guide, Your Counsel, Your Friend; you hold a measure of God's wisdom, strength, fortitude, courage, compassion, and love.

When you place God before you always, you are with God and God is with you.

From the Heart-connection of *Tiferet,* see God; open to God; come into God's holy, loving presence.

Chant:

שִׁוִּיתִי הִ׳ כְלַנֶגְדִּי תָמִיד

Shiviti Adonai L'negdi Tamid

I place God before me always.

שִׁוִּיתִי

הִ

ה

ו

ה

כְלַנֶגְדִּי

תָמִיד

Or: שְׁכִינָה *Shechinah*

Or: הַשֵׁם *HaShem*

Or: אָנֹכִי *Anochi*

I

place

G

O

D

before me

always.

—*Ps. 16:8*

2.

GEVURAH — STRENGTH

THE PLACE OF INGATHERING & BOUNDARIES
discernment / judgment

Coming Into God's Protection

"Good fences," the poet Robert Frost wrote, "make good neighbors."

Sometimes, fences keep out the unneeded and unwanted; sometimes, fences hold in and guard the precious.

As you move from the Heart Space of connection toward the conversation that you will soon have with God, you open yourself more and more. You want to know that the safety and integrity of your journey is assured.

You come from *Tiferet* to *Gevurah,* because *Gevurah* provides strength for the journey. It is not the masculine-like strength of power or brute force, but rather the feminine strength of resolute fortitude, of determination, and dependability. It is the strength that builds the fence — that takes in, and nurtures, and protects, and holds, and cherishes the most treasured.

Here in *Gevurah* is where your protective fence rises, for you can move forward toward God abiding only within the purest of the pure. After all, here you are very vulnerable. When you enter Sacred Space, you come out of your place, and you hover between Earth and Heaven. You need to be confident that there will be no outside interference, no outside force that tries to sabatoge your encounter with God. You need to know that the space you are in will be kept pure.

And, so you come to *Gevurah* where the clear lines, the good boundaries, the encompassing fence, can be drawn, so that you are with God in pure, uncompromised space.

Gevurah's overseer is the Archangel *Gavriel*—the only female of all the Archangels—who watches over purification. She is most welcome and celebrated at this *sefirah*, for this is the place where you invoke the purity of your journey to God.

With the psalmist of old, rejoice in saying, since "God is my shepherd-caretaker, I lack nothing." "I dwell in God's house." (Ps. 23: 6) I place myself in God's care.

In God's house, in God's care, I know that there is purity of being, purity in relationship. I know there is ultimate protection and enduring love.

And, from being in God's house of protection, care, and love, here, in my Earth-abode, I become more fully aware that all relationships have the capacity to evoke Sacred Space; that every relationship is in need of protective purity; and that I can do my part to ensure that the space of all my relationships is pure and protected.

And, when I am called to protect and care for my children, spouse, elderly parents, friends, employees, or community, by imitating God, I know how to be the very best protector and caretaker I can be.

From the sheltering boundaries of *Gevurah*, feel God's protection, feel God's care, feel God's love.

Chant:

וְשַׁבְתִּי בְּבֵית ה'

V'shavti b'veit Adonai

Or: שְׁכִינָה *Shechinah*

Or: הַשֵּׁם *HaShem*

Or: אָנֹכִי *Anochi*

I place mySelf

in

God's care.

—Ps. 23:6

3.

CHESED — UNCONDITIONAL LOVE

THE PLACE OF BOUNDLESS OUTREACHING
covenantal, providential love and compassion

Feeling God's Love

Once your heart is open at *Tiferet,* and you feel protected and cared for in *Gevurah,* you come into *Chesed* in relaxed confidence. You come to feel God's love, and to be filled up with God's love.

"How do I love thee?"

It is a good question to ask human beings who love—or choose, or reject, or demand, or withhold love—in countless ways.

For God, there is one and only one answer.

God says: I love you fully, completely, unequivocally, without condition, without reservation, without judgment. God loves us—you, and every being—with, in the words of the traditional morning prayer, *chen, va'chesed, v'rachamim,* most commonly translated as "grace, lovingkindness, and mercy."

You've perhaps heard a sweet little child described as *chenadick,* full of grace. Grace is God's total, complete acceptance of you, no matter who you are or what you do. It's God's providence. You don't have to do anything to receive God's grace, God's embrace, because as a child of God, you get it—automatically and irrevocably.

And *chesed* is most often translated as "lovingkindess." But, *chesed* is more accurately translated as "unconditional, covenantal love." Like grace, God gives it and you get it automatically, just because God is God, and you are you. There is no condition, no test. You are God's child, and God loves you.

And, God gives *rachamim*—commonly translated as "mercy," but really meaning "deep, deep compassion." *Rachamim* is more complicated than *chen* or *chesed,* which you get automatically. For, God has a choice. Within God is both the attribute of compassion, and the attribute of justice. God can give you either. It is always a Divine balancing act—justice or mercy. For God, it is a constant struggle. That is why the Talmud says that God's prayer to GodSelf is: "May it be My will that My attribute of mercy outweigh My attribute of strict justice." So, you ask of God infinite compassion. And God is gentle with you.

And then you, who are created in the image of God, are to imitate God. You are to be in dialogue with God, to be guided by God, to learn from God, how to offer your own *chen, va'chesed, v'rachamim.*

First, to God.

It can't be easy being God. Just think of what God hears everyday. "Please God, let my team win; no, God, let my team win. Please bring rain for the crops; no, please bring sunshine for the picnic. Please God, let my mother, my father, my child live. Upset the natural order for me; change the inevitable cycle of life and death so that my request is honored."

When something bad happens, we are often quick to blame God. How could God let this happen? How could a loving God let this be?

When your prayers are not answered the way you wish, you may be quick to denounce or abandon God. But, you can't love God on condition, any more than you want God to love you on condition. Give God your *chen,* your automatic grace; give God your *chesed,* your unconditional love; give God your *rachamin,* your gentle, infinite compassion.

And, then, give your *chen, va'chesed, v'rachamim* to every person you know, every person you meet, every person whose life touches yours. The heart of the world is open. It can be filled with chaos and toxins. Or, it can be filled with unconditional love and grace, with the never-ending flow of infinite compassion.

Now, admittedly, this is not easy. You are not God, who accepts all children with unconditional love. You are often bothered by people; you don't like some people very much; you think some people are strange, or unpleasant, or downright dangerous. It is hard to be non-judgmental; to offer automatic acceptance, and unconditional love.

But, you can try. You can try to give your *chen* and your *chesed* without condition.

Our sages taught that you can manifest your *chesed*, your unconditional love, by doing acts of *chesed*.

Everyday, you can do small, simple acts of kindness. Give the work of your hands. Help a young, overwhelmed mother feed the baby. Take her older children to the park. Give a ride to an older person who cannot drive anymore. Pick up a prescription for someone who is ill. Make her a meal. Sit and listen to a friend who is sad. Visit a friend who is lonely. Say hello to a stranger who is lost. "F.A.N.A.M.I."— "Find a Need and Meet It." The needs are great; the ways to help are endless. Reach out to another human being who needs you. Do a *chesed*, and enrich the world.

And, then, like God, you can choose to give your *rachamim*. Your soul is God's; and your body is of God's making. But your heart is yours. You decide what to do with your heart. You choose.

Your heart can be hard, and distant, and cold, or it can be open, and warm, and inviting. It can be rigid in strict judgment, or it can be filled with sweet compassion. In the words of the psalmist, you strive to get " a heart of wisdom." (Ps. 90:12) A wise heart chooses God; a wise heart chooses to be in alignment with God's design, so that compassion can flow from your heart into the heart of everyone you know.

One more thing. Give your *chen, va'chesed, v'rachamim* to yourSelf. Who's harder on you than you? Be gentle with yourSelf. Give yourSelf total and complete acceptance; your own non-judgmental, unconditional love; be compassionate with yourSelf. Surely, you have your flaws, and failings, but, you don't become a better person, by beating yourself up; you don't improve your life by tearing yourself down. You become a better person, you make this world better, through *chen, va' chesed, v'rachamim*.

From the grace, love, and compassion of *Chesed*, open your heart; enlighten your eyes; do and be *chesed*.

Chant:

חֵן וְחֶסֶד וְרַחֲמִים

Chen, Va'Chesed, V'Rachamim

Grace,

and

Love,

and

ComPassion

—*The morning prayer,* Sim Shalom

4.

NETZACH—EVERLASTING ENDURANCE
THE PLACE OF OUTWARD CREATIVE ENERGY
the male aspect / expansion and increase

Toning the Vibration of God's Love

The *Seraphim,* the greatest of all the Angels, live in the very Highest of the Heavens, surrounding the Throne of God.

Their singular and most holy task is to be responsible for all vibrations, all wave motions—all colors, all sounds, all frequencies—throughout creation.

They stand on every side of God's Throne, and they praise God by chanting across the Heavens—*"Kadosh, Kadosh, Kadosh.* Holy, Holy, Holy. The whole Earth is filled with God's glory."

They chant and chant *"Kadosh"* over and over, again and again. Always. Forever.

And, out of that sacred chanting, that holy toning, emerges the great Love Vibration that is the Source of All Creation, the Substance of All Form.

Joyously, the *Seraphim* sing: *"Kadosh, Kadosh, Kadosh.* Holy, Holy, Holy is the Lord of Hosts."

Their praise of God infuses the whole universe.

And here on Earth, you hear the angels, and, you too, want to praise God. So, you, who are just a little lower than the angels, rise up on your toes, so you can be as close to them as you can. And you joyously sing: *"Kadosh, Kadosh, Kadosh.* Holy, Holy, Holy is the Lord of Hosts. The whole Earth is filled with God's glory." You reverberate the Love Vibration.

And, very pleased and grateful, God listens.

And, then, God responds. God, too, sings: *"Kadosh, Kadosh, Kadosh.* Holy, Holy, Holy. The whole Earth is filled with God's glory." The Love Vibration suffuses Creation.

The song of God's holiness, the Love Vibration, fills every space in the universe; it traverses all time, and echoes to eternity.

God is the Love Vibration.

And you are the Love Vibration.

God's love, your love, expands and expands, grows greater and greater, and fills the entire cosmos.

All is Love. Love is All.

Here in *Netzach*, where creative energy increases and expands continually outward, even to the far reaches and expanses of creation, your affirmation of the Ever-Enduring God, your expression of your love for God, stretches to infinity.

Every breath of every living being; every breath of the whole world; every place, every moment, every one is *"Kadosh, Kadosh, Kadosh;" "Sanctus, Sanctus, Sanctus;"* "Holy, Holy, Holy."

Everything is God.

Everything is Love.

From the Love Vibration of *Netzach*, embrace the angels; sing holy love into and out from your whole being; feel the flow of God's love and yours fill the whole universe.

Chant:

קָדוֹשׁ קָדוֹשׁ קָדוֹשׁ

Kadosh, Kadosh, Kadosh

Holy,

Holy,

Holy

—*Isaiah 6:3 & daily liturgy,* Kedushah

5.

HOD — GLORY

THE PLACE OF INNER CREATIVE ENERGY
the female aspect / contraction and intensity

Becoming One with the Breath of God

At the moment of creation, *Ruach Elohim*, "the breath, the spirit, of God" hovered over the waters. At the moment of the creation of *Adam Kadmon*, the very first human being, God "blew into his nostrils the breath of life, and he became a living soul." (Gen. 2:7)

The breath of God is the life-force of human beings. You exist, you live, because your breath is the Breath of God. "You send forth Your Breath, O God, and we are created. You take away our breath and we die and return to the dust."

It is easy to pay little heed to your breathing; it is easy to take your breathing for granted. But, when you are mindful of your breathing, when you pay close attention to each breath, when you listen carefully and hear your breath within you, you can become very aware of God within you.

The very word for breath, *Ruach*—pronounced *Roo-ach* (the *ach* is a guttural as in Johann Sebastian B*ach)*—sounds the whoosh of air, the InBreath and OutBreath of natural breathing.

In *Hod*—the place of coming inward to be in the quiet realm of inner energy—when you breathe with full cognizance and intention, you can merge your breath with God's Breath. That puts you in close connection with God, and attuned to God's harmonic ebb and flow for the universe.

And, there is more. Not only are you in touch with God Within, but you are the complete partner with God in breathing the Being-ness of the entirety of creation.

God breathes God's Breath; you breathe your breath. But, the breaths are not individual; they are not separate. You and God share one breath; you breathe the same breath together. God's OutBreath is your InBreath. Your InBreath is God's OutBreath. Can you imagine anything more intimate, anything more ardent?

And what does this in-sync breathing do? It breathes the Love Vibration into every cell of your being, and into every space and place in creation.

You become like the *Seraphim,* who continually praise God by chanting "*Kadosh,*" and send the Love Vibration into the world. Your whole being becomes *Hod,* the glorious praise of God; and the Love Vibration transmigrates through you.

You become like God, sustaining life through the act of breathing, and, with your breath, sending the Love Vibration to infuse all existence.

From the deep inner creative energy of *Hod,* breathe the life-force; breathe of God and with God; and bring the Love Vibration into your being and into all of creation.

Chant:

רוח

Ruach

Spirit / Breath of God

—after Genesis 1:2 & 2:7

6.

BINAH — UNDERSTANDING

THE PLACE OF DIRECT, FELT-SENSE EXPERIENCE
intuitive knowing

Being God's Co-Creative Partner

In almost all the ancient creation myths, before a god could create, s/he had to fight, battle, and defeat other gods in order to earn the right to be the creator. The mightiest, the most strategically clever, the most wily, prevails, "wins," and creates.

Not so in the Hebrew Bible's story of creation. There, the record of creation begins, "And God *said.* . . ." (Gen.1:3)

Later the New Testament affirms this model of creation with the statement, "In the beginning was the Word."

To create, God became not belligerent nor bellicose; not large nor intimidating. Rather, God contracted inward to focus on intuitive felt-sense; to ingather purpose; to pull Intention into the deepest center.

The Word is all-powerful. The Word of Creation is filled with the knowing of All That Is.

You say *Baruch She'amar;* "Praised is the One who spoke." I acknowledge within You, O God, the power and the glory to create worlds out of words.

And you know that, as God's co-creative partner, you, too, have the power to make—or break—worlds with your words.

With your breath in-sync with God's Breath, you come to speak words not of division but of unity; not of war, but of peace; not of hate, but of love.

And you know that whole worlds—the world of nations, of your community, of your commerce, of your home and family, and of your heart—depend, ultimately, on the words you speak. So, you are always very careful with your words. You "watch" your words and "weigh" your words; you know the grand power of the "words of your mouth."

And, there is more.

Creation comes from "the Void." Only in that dark, hidden place—God's inward contraction; the womb of a mother; the underground of a planted seed—can creation begin and growth result. The Void is not empty; it is full of potentiality. It is not to be feared or avoided; it is to be embraced and celebrated.

You come into true co-creative partnership with God when you go into God's Void; when you go to the "inside of the inside." That is how you align your being with the Divine design.

The every-moment continuing act of creation depends on you dancing with God. God moves right; you move left. God moves forward; you move back. Or, better, you "stand on God's feet"—like a little girl whose daddy is teaching her to dance—and you move as one. You and God are in complete balance. The interdependency between you and God is total.

Together, you and God crystalize the Intentions that will find form in the Words—for continuing creation, continuing revelation, the continuing movement toward ultimate redemption.

Together—from your *kavannah,* your spiritual intent—you and God speak worlds into Being.

From the Intention of *Binah,* hear the Word and know what is; dance with the WordSmith and know what can be; focus your intention, form your Word, and it shall be.

Chant:

בָּרוּךְ שֶׁאָמַר וְהָיָה הָעוֹלָם

Baruch She'amar v'hayah haOlam

Praised is the One Who spoke,

and the World came to be.

Praised is the One.

—*morning blessings*

7.

CHOCHMAH — WISDOM

THE PLACE OF CONSCIOUS INTELLIGENCE
contemplation / thought

Co-Creating God's Worlds

From the Void comes the Word. Now, the Word needs to come forth into the world; to be spoken; to be actualized; to turn the intuitive felt-sense of creation into the conscious reality of creation.

Binah intuits; *Chochmah* acts. *Binah* says, "I feel. Therefore, I Am." *Chochmah* says, "I think. Therefore, I Am." The active male energy of *Chochmah* effectuates *Binah's* In-Sight.

When you come into *Chochmah,* you join *Chochmah* in saying, "The Word goes forth from this time and place." You are the co-creator of God's worlds.

In *Chochmah,* you first speak your humble gratitude to God. "Thank You for fashioning and creating me. Thank You for the birth-gift of my pure soul and spirit; my mind, and heart. Thank You for the intricate and complex operations of my body, which animate and propel my being. For it is revealed and known to You that if even one of my pipes, or channels, or passages of my body were broken or out of order—if that which is to be open were closed; or that which is to be closed were open—I could not survive and serve You in the fullness of my being. In this and every moment, I am ever-grateful for Your all-wise protection and care."

Now, it is time for the Word to go out to the world.
When does a creation need the most compassion, the most love?
When it goes out on its own.

It was when the Word went forth, that the world—new and un-formed, fragile and delicate—needed God's most loving compassion, and received it in the form of the Garden and the Tree.

It is when your children go out with their new driver's licenses, or off to college, or on a cross-country trek, that you most want to wrap them in your deepest love and your infinite compassion.

The continuing manifesting of the Word depends on the benevo-lence and the graciousness of the One who speaks.

How shall the Word travel?

It can be clothed only in the finest and most impeccable garb. It can be spoken only in the sweetest voice. It can be wrapped only in the holy hands of deepest compassion. It can flow only on the Love Vibration.

That is how God does it.

So, in the full confidence of your rightful place as God's partner, when you co-create with God, you are aware that the words you speak create whole worlds. You say to yourSelf: "Let my intentions be spoken with compassion. Let my words be love; let my words be holy. Let my worlds be good."

You are well aware of what happens when the Word becomes tainted, when it is not held in the utmost honor. Sometimes, you for-get that we all are creatures of the One; sometimes, you harm the mag-nificent creation you have been given; sometimes, when you separate yourSelf from the Divine design, you threaten the well-being—and the very future—of creation HerSelf.

So, you say to God: "You are My Creator; I am of Your making. So, even if I seem unworthy, even if, now and then, my errors—inten-tional or unwitting—put the multi-faceted tapestry of creation into danger, please God, since I am Your handiwork, if not for my sake, then for Yours, have compassion on me.

"Open my eyes, and my ears, and my voice wide enough to hear and speak the Word, to cover the Word in love. Open my heart and my soul wide enough to acknowledge that 'The beginning of wisdom is the awe of God.'"

From the co-creating world of *Chochmah*, thoughtfully and wisely bring creation into Being; clothe creation in loving compassion; be embraced by the ever-enduring compassion of your Creator.

Chant:

הַנְּשָׁמָה לָךְ

וְהַגּוּף פָּעֳלָךְ

חוּסָה עַל עֲמָלָךְ

HaNeshamah Lach
V' ha goof pa-aLach
Chusah al ahmaLach

You created my soul,

And my body, too

Please God, Please God,

Have compassion with me.

—*High Holiday liturgy*

8.

YESOD — FOUNDATION

THE LIFE FORCE

grounding / balance / harmony / synthesis / connection

Manifesting God's Design

In *Binah,* the Word is intended and formed; in *Chochmah,* it is sent forth. Now, in *Yesod,* it manifests in your world.

You know *Yesod* well, for it is the place of your hunger, your thirst, your sexual drives, your will to survive. It is the "juicy-ness" of your life.

There are some faith traditions that teach that the highest form of spirituality is to withdraw from the world, to resist physical need. Not so, Judaism. Judaism teaches that this physical world, even with its temptations and its excesses, is a glorious place to be. It is where life is lived. And life should be lived to its fullest. You jump right into the arena, with all its charms and allurements, all its problems and its challenges, all its messiness and its grandeur.

A long-ago sage taught that the first question you will be asked when you leave this world and arrive on the Other Side is, "Were there any of the permissible Earthly pleasures that were available to you, in which you did not partake?" The second question — equally indicative of your participation in this world — will be, "Were you honest in your business dealings?"

In your *Yesod* engagement with the world, you also take responsibility for the well-being of our planet and all who live here. You use your Earth-energy to bring *tikkun*-healing, balance, and transformation to every place and every person, so that Earth can be Eden once again.

Your challenge—that which tests and defines your human-ness and your humane-ness—is how you balance and harmonize the physical world and the world of the spirit.

Yesod—your life-force and the place where you live—is the anchor to the physical world, the foundation that gives grounding and form to God's manifest reality. It is God "in-form-ation." It is God saying, "I Am here, affirming the relationship between us, bringing My Word into creation."

Your deepest knowing tells you: There is a place called the "Un-Manifest." It is where all units of knowledge reside. Waiting.

In order for anything to be created, it must be called forth from the UnManifest into the Void. In the Void, the place of creating, the *Seraphim* give it its vibration, and the *Chayot HaKodesh,* the Holy Animators, give it form, so that it can come into the world.

What calls something from the UnManifest into the Void?

Your prayers.

You create the world though your prayers—your connection and communication with God. For, it is in *Binah's* Void where God intends and forms, and, then sends the Intention into the *Chochmah*-place of being called forth. From there, it comes into the manifestation-reality of *Yesod.*

So, you pray, and, when you pray, God can be God. What happens, the old legend asks, to all the prayers of all the people? Angels stand on the sides of the Heavenly Throne, and catch all the prayers that are sent to God. The angels then weave all the prayers into a crown, which they place on God's head. God's sovereignty, God's manifest Godness, comes from you.

And, God responds. When you pray something from the Un-Manifest into the Void, 100 percent of the time, your prayer is answered.

That is why, in *Yesod,* you say, "O God, who hears prayer, please listen to my prayer." For, your prayer begins the process that creates, and forms the foundation of worlds.

The truth is that God does not always answer your prayer the way you might hope—the way you prayed. For God is the only One who knows how your prayer fits into the Divine blueprint, the ultimate plan, the greatest good.

But, God always listens, and God always responds. And your prayer is the catalyst that sets worlds into motion.

From the *Yesod* place of manifestation, be well-grounded and in place, pray well; revel in the design of creation.

Chant:

שׁוֹמֵעַ תְּפִילָה

Sho'me-ah tefilah

O, please God,

Please listen.

Please listen,

Listen to my prayer.

—daily liturgy and, notably
the High Holiday prayer, Hinneni

9.

THE BACK OF DA'AT

THE ENTRANCE INTO GOD'S TIME TUNNEL AT THE HIGH HEART
being ever-present

Coming Into Perfect Alignment with God

Since the fall, the separation, the exile, from Eden, human beings on Earth have yearned to return to the paradise of perfection—of complete and total Oneness.

Da'at, which resides at the High Heart—the seat of spirit in the human form—is the place of perfect alignment with God. It is the Time Tunnel of return.

Da'at has been hidden away from us—and, thus, is known as the "shadow *sefirah*," and is often depicted with broken lines—because the pathway to return has been closed to us.

Now, it becomes accessible, and we may once again come into perfect alignment with the Divine.

You enter into the back of the Time Tunnel of *Da'at*. *Emet*, the full truth of All That Is, flows through. In its flow, you shape the truth in accordance with who you are, and so become the perfect co-creative partner with God. Because from the front of *Da'at*, the new truth, shaped by you, will emerge.

When Moses stood at the Burning Bush, God was in the midst of the flame, ready to give Moses his mission. God was present at the Time Tunnel, calling Moses in.

But, Moses was a reluctant prophet. He did not want the job of bringing the Hebrews out of Egyptian slavery. God's every assurance seemed not enough to satisfy or convince Moses. He offered every excuse and rationale to say to God, "No. Not I."

With almost every objection answered, and the inevitable looming, Moses asked, "When I come to the children of Israel, and say to them, The God of your fathers sent me, and they say to me, What is His name? what shall I say?"

"And God said, tell them, *'Eh-yeh Asher Eh-yeh.* I Am That I Am.'" (Ex. 3:13-14)

God identifies GodSelf as Infinity—"I Am. I Was, I Am, I Always Will Be. In Me is the wholeness, the totality, the Oneness of Everything That Is."

"I Am."

The "I Am" presence is God.

Now, you stand at the Burning Bush. God calls you in: I Am here. Now, you come here. Come into the *Da'at* Time Tunnel. Bring your truth to mix with My eternal truth, so that, through your prism, a new truth will emerge for a new world.

I Am the "I Am" presence.

You are the "I Am" presence.

The "I Am" presence is God.

The "I Am" presence is God Within you.

The modern "philosopher" Woody Allen said, "Ninety percent of life is showing up."

The Back of *Da'at* is where you and God "show up."

Be there.

Be ever-present.
Come into the Time Tunnel of *Da'at*.
Come into the "I Am" presence.
Come into perfect alignment with God, with the full truth of All That Is.

From the Back of *Da'at's* Time Tunnel, be called, accept the mission, and enter.

Chant:

אהיה אשר אהיה

Eh-yeh Asher Eh-yeh

I Am

I Am

I Am That I Am

—*Exodus 3:14*

10.

MALCHUT — KINGDOM

also known as the *sefirah* of the

SHECHINAH — THE INDWELLING FEMININE

MANIFEST MATERIALITY
rootedness / relationship / union / shelter / nurture

Being in Oneness with God

Listen up! Pay attention!
>Jews. And All People, Everywhere

יהוה *Yud, Hey, Vav, Hey. Yahweh. Adonai.* (translated into English as "Lord")
>who was, is, and ever will be,

Is our God.
>among all who claim to be Divine; among the pretenders, and the "wanna-bes,"

יהוה *Yud, Hey, Vav, Hey. Yahweh. Adonai.* (the Lord)
Is One.
>Singular. Unique. Indivisible.

Our God — יהוה *Yud, Hey, Vav, Hey. Yahweh. Adonai* — is One. Our God's universe is One; our God's people are One.

And we are One with our God, with the universe, with all people.

This simple yet profound statement — known as the *Sh'ma Yisrael* — is Judaism's clear, concise, unequivocal declaration of faith, and one of the central, core prayers of the Jewish worship service.

Sh'ma Yisrael is spoken in *Malchut*, the very, very root of the Tree of Life. It is here where the great weave of manifested materiality expresses the Divine spiritual intention.

What is the Divine spiritual intention?

"Material," from the Latin *"mater,"* is the mother—the feminine that is the physical, the manifest. *Malchut* is the realm of the *Shechinah,* the Divine feminine. So, *Malchut/Shechinah* holds all manifestation of all creation within its being. The entirety of All—and, surely, all the *sefirot* which represent All—is within *Malchut.* And since *all* matter is made of the Love Vibration, then All is One.

Malchut is spirit in matter. It is the place where the transcendent God comes to meet you on Earth—in your physical world. Here, together, God and you declare the Oneness of All That Is.

You declare: יְהֹוָה *Yud, Hey, Vav, Hey. Yahweh. Adonai* is our God—One, Alone. And you are One with all of Divine creation.

You already know this at the depth of your being, for the Oneness of All is a piece of eternal knowledge that you carry with you always. The recitation of *Sh'ma Yisrael* is your rational mind calling up and affirming what your soul memory holds.

And there is more. For *Sh'ma Yisrael* is not only a cognitive, rational statement of belief. It can also be the Jewish mantra.

Repeated over and over again—prohibited by some traditionalists; but embraced by those who understand the powerful litany and rhythm of prayer—you can use the chant of *Sh'ma Yisrael* to bring you closer and closer, to help you connect with God.

Reciting *Sh'ma Yisrael* over and over again has the soothing and compelling purpose of quieting your mind, focusing your attention, and helping you move from the level of mundane thought to the level of higher consciousness. It is a way of meditatively moving into God-space, of finding and sustaining your connection to God, of entering into God's holy presence, and of coming into deep conversation and intimate relationship with God.

"I call to You, O God, to come be with me, and ask You to invite me to be with You; to fill me with Your Light and Your Love. I feel complete unity with You, and with every human being, with every living thing on Earth, with the stars and the planets, and every particle of Your creation."

Sing *Sh'ma Yisrael* in its well-known, popular American melody. Or, better, sing it in the original Torah cantillation. Feel the power of the music itself embracing the words—its poignant sound resonating across the millennia; its rich desert-like sound vibrating deep within you; its ancient sound as familiar as your own name, as intimate as a lover's gentle caress.

Chant *Sh'ma Yisrael,* three, or seven, or ten, or forty times. Over, and over, and over again. Let the power of repetitive chant do its work of connecting you and God.

As with the rational declaration of faith that calls up your eternal knowledge that All is One, here, the constant repetition of Oneness brings you back to the place from where you know and remember blissful Oneness—God's holy presence.

Some ask how it is possible to get caught up in the chant, without, at the same time, being distracted by counting to seven or forty.

In his book, *The Seventh Telling: The Kabbalah of Moshe Katan,* Rabbi Mitchell Chefitz teaches this simple meditative technique.

If you decide to chant *Sh'ma Yisrael* seven times for example, in your mind's eye, build a little two-tiered box of seven blocks.

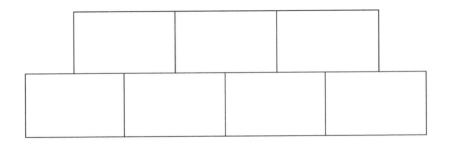

When you chant *Sh'ma Yisrael* the first time, light a flame—a Burning Bush—in the first box.

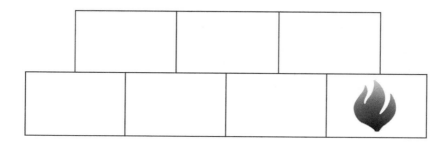

Each time you chant *Sh'ma Yisrael*, light another flame in another box.

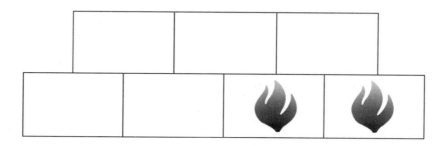

When you reach seven chants, your flame box will be filled.

At first, you will be thinking about the boxes and the flames, but, soon your flame lighting—and your numbered chanting—will become automatic.

Calling God's Name, in mantra-like focus, celebrates God's Oneness, affirms your own Oneness, and asks God to be in relationship with you—to open the mystical pathway for you to be in conversation with God. It asks God to be your Friend, your Counsel, your Comfort, your Guide.

From *Malchut's* manifest materiality of all creation, feel God's all-enveloping presence, be bathed in God's radiant light, let your heart and soul be touched by God's love.
You are with God.

Chant:

שְׁמַע יִשְׂרָאֵל ה' אֱלֹהֵינוּ ה' אֶחָד

Sh'ma Yisrael Adonai Elohenu Adonai Echad

Or: שְׁכִינָה *Shechinah*

if you choose to call God Shechinah, *then instead of saying* אֶחָד Echad, *the masculine form of One, say* אַחַת Achat, *the feminine form of One.*

Or: הַשֵּׁם *HaShem*

Or: אָנֹכִי *Anochi*

Listen, all People!

The Lord is our God.

The Lord is One.

Or: הֹ׳ *Adonai*

Or: שׁכִינָה *Shechinah*

Or: הַשֵּׁם *HaShem*

Or: אָנֹכִי *Anochi*

—Deut. 6:4

11.

KETER—CROWN

THE DWELLING PLACE OF GOD &
THE UNION WITH GOD

THE PLACE WHERE MATTER AND SPIRIT MEET,
WHERE MATTER BECOMES SPIRIT

transcendence / illumination / revelation

Communicating with God

You have journeyed through the magical pathways of the Spiral Tree of Life, drinking in the energies of each of the *sefirot,* savoring the unique encounter with God at each emanating step.

Now, from *Malchut,* you spiral up the entire Tree of Life in one leaping spin. You zoom from the bottom of the Tree of Life to its very top.

You go from where God meets you on Earth where you dwell—spirit in matter—to where you meet God where God dwells—matter in spirit.

You are with God in *Keter,* the place of ultimate union, of complete Oneness.

You have come to be with God.

In the traditional worship service, this is the place and the time of the *Amidah* (which means "standing," because, the sages taught, when you come before the holy God, you stand in respect and reverence.) This lengthy, fixed prayer—which reflects much of the human condition in relationship to the Divine—was inserted into the service to give you words to say to God, in case you have no words of your own to say.

Whether you are more comfortable standing or sitting when you talk to God, this is the place where your spiral spiritual practice has been leading you. This is the time of your deep meditation, your own intimate conversation with God.

Rabbi Aryeh Kaplan *zt"l* taught, "All references to meditation vanished from mainstream Jewish literature about 150 years ago. . . . [But] there is a strong tradition of meditation and mysticism . . . in mainstream Judaism. . . . [And] since Judaism is an eastern religion that migrated to the west, its meditative practices may well be those most relevant to western [wo]/man."

In meditation, you have come to talk to God, and to listen as God talks to you.

You are in God's holy presence. It is awesome and glorious. And it can be daunting and, even, intimidating, for you are—as the philosopher tells it—in "fear and trembling." You are acutely aware that "there is an Eye that sees, and an Ear that listens." (Avot 2:1)

And, it is, at the same time, warm, and welcoming, and very, very comfortable. You are Home. The transcendent God—the God of the entire cosmos—is also the immanent God, with you and within you. *Ein Sof,* the Infinite God who fills the whole universe, envelops you—you, alone—in the most loving embrace. You speak, and the Ineffable Almighty—who is lonely without you—joins you in intimate conversation. God speaks, and the Divine utterance is your very own lovesong.

In the language of the Kabbalah, here in the *Keter* place of union, you seek to merge with God; you seek *devekut,* to cleave to, to blend, to meld with God.

If, as Martin Buber taught, you can be in deep, merged, intimate "I-Thou" relationship with another human being, then, surely, you can be in deep, merged, intimate "I-Thou" relationship with the "Eternal Thou"—God.

You do this through *hitbodedut,* "self-isolation," or, better, "isolation from Self." You go to your deepest place, the place of the "inside of your insides," the place beyond ego and identity.

You say, "Hello God." "I just called to say I love You. And I mean it from the bottom of my heart."

And God says, "Hello, my precious child." "You just call out My Name, and you know wherever I am, I'll come running, and I'll be there. You've got a friend." "It is so good to be with you, so sweet to talk with you."

You are in *yichud,* your deep, intimate alone time with God.

When you are with God, you connect the Divine that is Within you with its Divine Source. The "holy sparks" of God that are within you meet their Origin, and God's Light of creation from where they were kindled is, in turn, re-enflamed.

When you are with God, you are in the magnificence of total, absolute, Love. God is Love. You are Love. Together, you and God are the greatest of all Love.

You talk and God listens.

What do you say?

Sometimes, it takes only one word, for in the intimacy of the embrace of love, even in one word, whole worlds are spoken and received.

Or, you can begin by saying:

I come to You, O God
to acknowledge You,
to bless You, to praise You,
and to thank You;
to
talk to You,
and to
listen
as You talk to me
in
the sweet and holy Voice
of
Your Word
and
Your Will.

Then, say anything and everything. Pour out your heart and cry out your soul to the Creator of your heart and soul. Sing your joy. Shout. Whisper. Argue. Wrestle. Be guided. Be challenged. Be comforted. Be enlightened.

In the form of traditional prayer, you may want to:

Praise.

> In your own words, and through your own experiences, you may want to say, "How great are Your works, O God. The whole Earth is filled with Your glory." I am in awe.

Thank.

> In your own words, and through your own experiences, you may want to say, "It is good to give thanks to God . . . to declare Your lovingkindness . . . and Your faithfulness." Thank You, O God, for all Your many blessings of life and sustenance. I am in gratitude.

Does God need your praise and thanks? Probably not. But, even God likes to hear a good word now and then; God likes to know that God's God-ness and God-ing are appreciated.

But, even more, you need to praise and thank God for you. You need to remind yourSelf that it is not your might nor your power that moves and controls the universe. It is God's spirit. You need to be in humility, awe, and gratitude, so that you can say, with glad conviction, "God is God."

Ask.

> In your own words, and through your own experiences, you may want to ask God for what you want and desire— for you, for the ones you love, for your world. I am in need.

Surely, you can ask God for healing of body, mind, and spirit, for those in need and for yourSelf.

El, nah, r'fah nah lah. "Please, God, please heal her."

El, nah, r'fah nah lo. "Please, God, heal him."

El, nah, r'fah nah li. "Please, God, heal me."

Now, here comes the big, big learning:

It is perfectly proper to ask God to fulfill your needs and your desires. Yet, there are some "ground rules," some boundaries.

As the Talmud teaches, when you hear the fire bells in your town, you cannot pray that the fire is not in your house, because it is a prayer that is for naught. The bells are announing a fire that is already burning, and, God does not change the fire from one place to another, even for the most fervent plea.

And God does not provide red bicycles for good little children; parents do. God does not provides "A"s on tests; good studying students earn them. God does not provide victories for sports teams; good athletes prevail.

And God does not provide what God has already given us the ability to achieve by ourselves. As Rabbi Jack Riemer puts it, "We cannot merely pray to You, O God, to end war . . . to end starvation . . . to root out prejudice . . . to end despair . . . to end disease. For You have made the world in such a way that we must find our own path . . . to peace. . . . You have given us the resources to feed all people . . . to clear away the slums and give hope . . . to search out cures and healings. . . . Therefore, we pray 'to do' instead of only 'to pray.'"

Perhaps your prayer, then, should be for raising your consciousness—for the extending of your capacities and your abilities to see, and explore, and envision; for a greater measure of wisdom, and insight, and fortitude, and compassion. Your prayer can be for constant good counsel and guidance, so that you can turn the words you pray into the good work of transforming and perfecting a world that so desperately needs your heart and your hands. "May God's goodness be upon me and establish the work of my hands." (adapted from Ps. 90:17)

There is one more aspect to the big, big learning.

You always retain your persona, your essence, your full Self. Yet coming to God requires the stripping away of all ego, the stripping of all pretense, the utterly honest confrontation with all the aspects of Self—real and imagined; illuminated and shadow—that are within you. You fully surrender to God.

Often, in your prayers, you may try to convince God that your will—the things you want and desire—should be God's will.

But, God's world does not work that way.

God's values are supreme. They supersede your feelings, and your desires, and your cravings, and your choices—no matter how worthy and worthwhile your inclinations might be.

God's will is God's will.

Your view of the world is bounded by what you can see and experience at a given moment, and what you are able to possibly envision for future time. And, your world-view is greatly influenced by your very human needs and desires, and your very human feelings and emotions.

God's view of the world is unlimited. God "was, is, and always will be." God sees the past, the present, and the future of the entire cosmos. God, who created the universe and everything in it—including you—has a design, a blueprint, for its—and your—continuing existence, and determines how it will unfold.

God decides what is right or wrong; what is in the highest and best interest of our world—including what is in your highest good.

Even at God's most compassionate and merciful, God never promises an existence without suffering and pain, a life without trial and tribulation. God never promises that no one will get sick, or that anyone will live forever. Pain and suffering and the sometimes harsh vicissitudes of existence—as bewildering and tormenting as they can be—are part of life.

And even with God's strictest sense of justice, God never ordains that you should not experience deepest joy, greatest satisfaction, profound happiness, and richest contentment.

Yet, God never intends that for you to be happy means that you get whatever you want—whatever that might be—whenever you want it. Hedonism and self-gratification are not God's values. Happiness—while much desirable—is not the highest human purpose. Rather, God tells you, *Dos leiben es a chiyuv,* "this life is an obligation"—to be good and to do good; to feel a sense of responsibility for the well-being of every human being, and for the betterment of the world.

God, who is the Oneness and the Wholeness of existence, declares that human life holds the Oneness and Wholeness of Everything. It is a delicate balance between pain and joy, tragedy and triumph. Every human being experiences a measure of All.

Your prayer surely holds the power to energize and influence—and, certainly, to avert the severity of the decree. But, even the most fervent prayer cannot keep you from the Wholeness of life—from hurt, or from happiness.

So, sometimes, God does not answer your prayer the way you would hope and expect. God determines that your request—even though you may think so—may not be in your highest and best interest. Or, God determines that your request may be good for you, but may not fit into the plan and blueprint, the ultimate design, for the whole world. It may not be in the collective highest good.

As the famed rabbi and writer, Chaim Potok *zt"l* put it (in an era before egalitarian language), "The seeing of God is not like the seeing of man. Man only sees between the blinks. He does not know what the world is like during the blinks. He sees the world in pieces, in fragments. But God sees the world whole, unbroken."

If you had God's perspective, you would be able to see how your life—and your requests—fit into the Divine Design. You could know that your heartfelt prayers—even when it seems to you as if they are not heard—are, indeed, heard and honored, even if they cannot be fulfilled in the way you would like. You would know that when you experience the very real human emotions of pain, and anguish, and suffering, God weeps with you in your pain, and—whether or not it seems so to you at the moment—comforts you, and lifts you up out of the depths.

In the same way, when it seems to you as if your prayers are answered in the way you would like, when you experience great moments of joy, happiness, and contentment, then, too, those emotions are not sourced in your own will, but in God's will.

Your prayer is to be in alignment with the Divine plan, to do God's will, and to ask God to do God's will.

As the revered teacher Rabbi Dr. Abraham Joshua Heschel zt"l put it (in the same non-egalitarian language of his day), "Prayer is not man imposing his will on God. It is God imposing His will—and mercy—on man."

Or as President Abraham Lincoln put it, "I want to humbly pray that we are on God's side."

As it is put most succinctly, "Thy will be done."

"May the words of my mouth and the meditations of my heart be acceptable to You, O, God. Accept my prayerful meditation, and answer me with *Your* great mercy and *Your* saving truth."

Ken y'hi ratzon—"May it be *Your* will, O God."

Can you know anything of what God wants; can you know anything of God's ultimate plan for the universe? Can you know God's will?

Absolutely. For, as Dr. Heschel zt"l taught, "In every man's life, there are moments when there is a lifting of the veil at the horizon of the known, opening a sight of the eternal."

There are some parts of God's plan that you surely know.

You know that God loves all God's children. God does not "play favorites;" God loves each child equally and unconditionally. And just as no two children in a household relate in exactly the same way to mother and father, you know that there are myriad ways to relate to God—each one valid and worthy.

If you are, for example, joyously and determinedly Jewish, you recognize and appreciate your friends and colleagues and neighbors who are joyous and determined followers of other faiths and other paths. You are part of a living organism. Every part—the heart, the liver, the kidneys—is needed to function; each part is needed for its unique place and role. God loves—and needs—us all.

So, God says: Certainly, do not forsake, or harm, or kill each other in My Name. That is a complete perversion of Me. You are all My children. I love you all. Glorify Me by caring about and for each other.

And you know also that God loves good, not evil. God's will is to elevate the human spirit, not crush it; to sanctify life, not destroy it. God loves justice, and goodness, and righteousness, decency and dignity, kindness and caring, mercy and compassion.

And, most of all God loves love, because Love is All; All is Love.

And God says to you: I created you in My image. Imitate me. Do justice, love mercy, walk humbly, bring holiness, and, above all, love. Love your God; love your neighbor, love yourSelf.

Will God really listen as you talk? Can your prayers—your intimate conversations—influence the Divine design?

You cannot ask God to upset the natural order, or to change the inevitable cycle of life and death for you. Yet, as the Bratslaver Rebbe taught, "God listens to every word of prayer. No word goes to waste."

You already know that prayer sends energy into the universe. Like any other energetic force, prayer can and does move and influence. The object of your prayer—animate or inanimate, but all of God—can be radically affected by your prayer energy. Modern scientific research affirms what theologians have long known: prayer helps seeds grow in laboratory petri dishes; and prayer has the power to change the crystalline structure of water. Prayer helps heal post-surgical heart patients, even when the pray-er does not know for whom he is praying, and the patient does not know that she is the subject of prayer; and prayer can lessen the rate of big-city violent crime on hot summer days.

Your prayer—your thought wave, your intention—goes out to the universe and—like the one flap of the butterfly wing that changes everything—your prayer has the possibility of shaping whole worlds. God always listens to your prayer, and may be moved to Divine thought or action by your request.

And your prayer to God is, at the same time, your prayer to yourSelf. There is a moment at the deepest level when only you can bear witness. Your prayer turns you inward—you talk to yourSelf, to seek your own understanding and development, to hear your own response to your own needs. Your prayer can alter your own consciousness; it can bring change to the biology of your body for your own physical healing, and it can bring change to your own emotional and spiritual bodies for the ever-unfolding growth of your heart and soul.

So, in your prayer, you say to God and to yourSelf, "I want to stay in alignment with the Divine will; I want to stay in the flow of the Divine design. And, if I find mySelf disconnecting from God, separate from God, I want to do the *tikkun,* the healing, and the *t'shuvah* of return. 'Return me unto You, O God, and I will return.' I want to do the atonement that brings At-One-Ment. I want to be whole with God."

In the *yichud,* the alone time, of *Keter,* when you are in union with God, you speak the desires of your heart.

Eleh chamda libi. Chusa na, v'al na titaleim. "These are the desires of my heart. Please have compassion. Please do not turn away."

And what are the desires of your heart—especially when you are stripped of ego?

Money? Power? Prestige? Fame?

Your Earth-ness may call you to these temporal gratifications, but your soul calls you to the deepest desires of the human spirit.

You seek—in the words of the modern prayer—"purpose to your work, meaning to your struggle, and direction to your striving."

You seek to make your contribution to a just and peaceful world.

You seek the answers to the very questions with which you began the journey on the mystical spiral pathway to God—the questions of the quest for ultimate meaning.

In the *yichud* of *Keter,* you ask God all your questions:

Who are You?

Who am I?

From where have I come, and where am I going?

What is the purpose of my existence?

How do I think?

How do I know?

How do I know beyond knowing?

What do I believe?

How can I best communicate with You and hear Your word to me?

How do I best stay connected to You?

How can I best know Your grand design for the universe?

Why is there so much evil and suffering in the world?

How can a good and loving God permit evil to exist?

How can I best know Your plan for me?

What is my mission, my destiny?

How do I best live a life of meaning, and a life of worth?

How do I find and sustain true love?

How do I find and sustain true happiness?

How do I evolve in mind, in spirit, in consciousness?

How do I feel the deepest soul-satisfaction, and how do I find and fulfill the grandest desires of my heart?

What happens to me after I die?

At the depth of your soul memory, you already know all the answers to your questions. When you are with God, you are remembering what you already know. You are fully aware that the totality of eternal knowledge is within you; you know the entirety of All That Is. In your Heavenly remembering, some of the mysteries and the wonders of your Earth-life come into better focus and greater understanding.

Then, when you return from being with God in *Keter*, another speck of your Earth-knowing is illuminated; your God-ness is expanded.

And, when you are with God, ask God for the health, strength, and wisdom you need along the way; to do God's will with whatever gifts you are granted; to face the vicissitudes of life with dignity and courage; to make every moment a blessing.

You ask to serve; to do God's will in whatever form and format God deems best for you.

You ask to use the best that is within you, to serve God with all your heart.

"Purify my heart that I may serve You in truth."

"Purify my heart." Help me to rid mySelf of any ills that beset me: hatred, and bigotry, and envy, and jealousy. Help me bring my heart to compassion, and kindness, and love.

"To serve You." Not my own selfish needs; not my own ideas of what is best for me; not my Earthly cravings and desires. But to serve You, O God—to do Your will.

"In truth." Your truth; not the limited view of my experience, but the entirety of Your perspective; not the temporal boundaries of my finite existence, but the greatness and the grandeur of Your infinite and eternal reality.

And, help me enter *Da'at* so that Your truth and mine can be refined in the Tunnel of Time, and emerge as new truth for this new world.

And, when you are with God, you can pray for miracles, for God's strong and clear intervention into this world, to bring Light and Love to every corner of existence. "Just as You did miracles for our ancestors in days gone by, please do miracles for us in our time."

And when you are with God, you know that the veil between This Side and the Other Side is growing thinner and thinner. You know that your sojourn on Earth is but a moment in eternity. "A thousand years in Your sight, O God, is but a day; the days of our lives but a fleeting shadow." (Ps. 90:4)

You know that one day, this Earth-journey of your body and ego will end. Yet, as the Talmudic sage, Yose ben Abin taught, "The day of death is when two worlds meet with a kiss; this world going out, and the future world coming in." And the Chasidic Kotzker Rebbe added, "It is just a matter of going from one room to the other."

Your soul is eternal. The true essence of your being lives on forever. You are immortal.

When for this moment, you have spoken all your words to God, God will respond. Know this with every fiber of your being; have no doubt: God will respond.

So, listen, listen, listen as God talks to you.

What will God say?

That is between you and God, for your conversation is personal and intimate; it is between God and you, alone.

Yet, surely, there are a few things that God might say to every One of us.

For just like the prophets of old, you are a prophet. You stand at the bush, atop the mountain, in the sheltering cleft of the rock and the cave, at the foot of the Temple, in the stream of exile and return. Though they tried, the ancient rabbis and the sages—who, for their own power and adulation, insisted that individual prophecy died, and God's continuing revelation comes only through them—could not block your vision or silence your voice.

You are in God's holy presence; you are in intimacy with God. You are a pure channel of the *Ruach HaKodesh*, the Holy Spirit of God's word and will. God's continually unfolding revelation lives in you. Through you, God comes into this world.

So, God might say: I Am Within you. I Am your Being. I placed within you All That Is. So, pay attention to your intuition, and your sensory perception, and your deja vu, and your soul memory, and your daydreams, and your nightdreams, for through them, you will know Me. You will remember the secrets and the mysteries; you will remember your purpose and your mission. You will become more fully aware of how your own soul mission, your own soul contract fits into My Divine plan. Your soul will grow in wisdom and in love; the desires of your heart will be fulfilled.

God might say: I need you to help build up this world of Ours. We have a sacred task, and I rejoice that you are My co-creative partner. Please bring My message of healing and hope, and please inspire the holy work of billions of hearts and hands.

Most of all, know that I love you, and I cherish you, and I honor you, and I celebrate you, and I walk with you hand in hand through this journey of life. I Am with you always—in this our daily conversation, and whenever you call. For, like Me, yours is the power and the glory—and the unending love—forever and ever.

In his contemporary, best-selling book, *The Prayer of Jabez*, Bruce Wilkinson tells that when the time comes that you pass from this Earth to the Other Side, waiting for you will be a box with your name on it.

In the box will be God's answers to all the questions you never asked, God's responses to all the prayers you never prayed.

Our prayer is that your box will be empty.

That is why God says, "Do not be afraid." Speak and you shall be heard. Pray and you shall be answered. Ask, and you shall receive.

God invites you: Joyously join Me in *Keter*. Cleave to Me. Together we go to the "inside of the insides." Together, we find life's deepest meaning, most noble cause, greatest glory, and richest blessings.

And you say, "*Hineini*. Here I Am. I am ready."

From *Keter's* supremely sublime place of grand alone-ness, cleave to God, speak your words, listen to the Divine response, and revel in God's love.

Chant:

Hineini

Here I Am

—various Biblical passages,
including responses to God
from Abraham, Jacob, and Moses.

12.

THE FRONT OF DA'AT

THE EMERGING FROM GOD'S TIME TUNNEL WITH NEW-FOUND TRUTH AT THE HIGH HEART

weaving together diverse elements; braiding the male and female
into the full Self; shaping the experience of the Divine

Ever-Experiencing God and GodSelf

Oh, how good it would feel to stay in the sweet, womb-like cradle of God's holy presence, God's all-encompassing attention and protection, God's Light and Love.

You know that you can be in intimate conversation with God whenever you want. You call; God answers. You come; God welcomes. Return again, and again, says God.

As Reb Shlomo *zt"l* sings, "Return again. Return again. Return to the land of your soul. Return to who you are. Return to what you are. Return to where you are born and reborn again."

You will. Soon. Very soon.

But, now, your Earth-life beckons, it calls, it insists that you bring the God-energy forward into your daily life.

When Moses stood at the sea, with the churning waters in front of him and the Egyptian soldiers behind him, the Israelites cried out in prayer because they were afraid. God told Moses that there are times for prayer, and times for action. "Speak to the Children of Israel, and tell them to go forward." (Ex. 14:15)

There is a time for you to pray and talk to God, and there is a time to act—to get up, go forward, and build your world on Earth.

Now, in your daily spiritual practice is the time to to re-engage with life—even with all its uncertainties; surely with all its sorrows and its joys, its tragedies and its triumphs. Be in Earth's soaring beauty and her grand possibilities. Be in your responsibilities, and your pleasures, and your great loves. Be in your work here on Earth—being God's co-creative partner in healing and perfecting this world.

When you emerge—from this and every encounter with God—you know and feel God better than you did before. The desires of your heart have been spoken and heard. Another piece of the secrets of the universe has been revealed to you; you grasp an iota more of the mysteries of existence. You are enlivened and enriched. The God Within you is enlarged and extended; you are a more enLightened being.

You come forward into your Earth-life through the Time Tunnel of the Front of *Da'at*.

You have been shaped and enriched by your experience with God, just as God has been shaped and enriched by the experience with you. From what you discovered during your conversation with God, together, you and God see ancient truths through new prisms, and the new truths that emerge become part of All That Is. You emerge from the Front of *Da'at's* Time Tunnel with new truths that you take out to the world. Your personal communication with God adds new wisdom to the collective consciousness.

You, yourSelf, have become *sefirah*-like. You are a gateway for connection to God.

It is here, at the Front of *Da'at,* that the fullness of Source, all expressions of Source, are braided together into wholeness. Male and female, light and dark, captivity and freedom, hatred and love, war and peace; all the archetypes, all the Names and attributes of God, all your names and attributes—everything, everything—become One.

And what is the Name of the One, the fullness of Source, and the fullness of Source-God?

It is *Anochi*—"I"—the everything, the complete essence of God. The All That Is.

Anochi is God's "GodSelf." It is the "I-MySelf, wholeness of My Being; the Me-ness of Me. The Source and Substance of All."

And, *Anochi* is your "GodSelf;" the totality of God Within you.

All is One. One is All.

When you call God, *Anochi,* when you recognize the *Anochi Within,* you affirm the new truth that emerges from the Front of *Da'at.* You embrace the new truth that can—and will—make the world One.

From the Front of *Da'at,* emerge from being with God, be in your sacred life on Earth, bring the new emerging truths of the universe, and celebrate *Anochi,* the "I-Totality" of God, and the *Anochi Within* you.

Chant:

אָנֹכִי

Anochi

I

INTERLUDE

FOR

CELEBRATING SOULS IN THE LIGHT

In the inevitable ebb and flow of life, there will be times when you are mourning the death, or observing the yahrzeit *(the anniversary of the death) of a loved One.*

In your 20 MINUTE KABBALAH *prayers, you will want to remember and pay honor and tribute to the Ones who have gone from this Earth to the Great Beyond on the Other Side.*

All our Jewish lives, we have been told that when a close relative—parent, sibling, spouse, child—dies, we are to come to the synagogue to recite *kaddish.*

Kaddish, we are taught, is not a prayer about death, but a doxology, a prayer of praise to God. So, even in our grief, we are to stand up in the midst of our community—a *minyan,* a quorum of at least ten Jews—to declare our continuing faith in God and the Divine plan.

Kaddish is no ordinary prayer. Its words and litany, rhyme, and rhythm are part of the collective Jewish unconscious, part of the soul-self of our Beings. It holds the mystery and the magic of existence that come from before the beginning, and that will ripple until the end of time.

Kaddish is not only a faithful affirmation of God, but, also, words of condolence spoken directly to God. One of God's children has left this temporal Earthly world, and God, GodSelf, is bereaved. So, we offer our sympathy directly to God, who is mourning the Earthly-death of one of the Divine children. In the words of the famed writer of our people, Shmuel Yosef Agnon, as we say *kaddish,* "we pray for us, and for Him [God.]"

And, by coming to recite *kaddish,* we speak also to the soul of our loved one who has died. We say, "I will miss you, and I will always yearn for you, but, in submission and humility, with love and blessing, I release you and give you back to God. I assure myself and you that there is nothing to fear. As reluctant as I am to say this, and as reluctant as you are to hear this: Go. Go to the Light. Be wrapped in God's protecting love. Your precious soul will be safe and well in God's holy presence, for with God, all is good. And, in case you or I have any doubts I proclaim and affirm—for you and for me to hear—our ancient truth: 'Magnified and sanctified is the Great Name of God.'"

We come to recite *kaddish* for eleven months—from the time of the funeral until one month before the first *yahrzeit*, the first anniversary of the death.

During these eleven months, the regular recitation of *kaddish* helps us do what our ancients intuitively understood, and what modern psychology has termed, "grief-work "—the slow but deliberate process of mourning; of coming to full realization and the eventual, inevitable acceptance of the death of the one we love.

Why eleven months and not the full year?

Here enters the world of spiritual legend and lore (and some would say, superstition.) We are taught that in the year following death, our loved one's soul is being judged. Enough good deeds earns eternal reward; too many evil deeds means an extended time of separation from God. So, we learn that each time we recite *kaddish,* we are adding to our loved one's *"mitzvah* points," earning additional merit for one who might be deficient.

Yet, no one we love could be so evil that it would take a full year of earning more merit to achieve Paradise. Eleven months should be sufficient for even the most needing soul. Thus, we recite *kaddish* for but eleven months, confident that our Earthly assistance has been enough to assure that our loved one will enter eternal Eden.

Still, with all these worthy reasons for reciting *kaddish*—and even with all the compelling Jewish stories about the gathering of ten, and the waiting for the tenth so that a mourner can say *kaddish*—the reality is that most modern, liberal Jews do not regularly come to synagogue for the three daily services to recite *kaddish,* and many do not even come once a week on Shabbat. Surely, in this personal prayer-life of 20 MINUTE KABBALAH, you will most likely not be in a synagogue with a *minyan.*

Along with my rabbinic colleagues, I lamented the reality that the recitation of *kaddish* with a *minyan,* which only a generation ago, was one of the most widely observed Jewish ritual obligations, has largely fallen—no pun intended—into the graveyard of contemporary indifference.

And, then, my father died.

I was deeply committed to the idea of honoring my father through the daily recitation of *kaddish.* I am, after all, his *"kaddish-el,"* his son, whose duty and blessing it is to say *kaddish* for him.

Yet, even though I am deeply committed to daily prayer and meditation, I did not always go to synagogue for the thrice-a-day synagogue services, and I even found myself missing an occasional Shabbat service.

And since I was deeply imprinted with the Jewish mindset that *kaddish* may be recited only in a *minyan,* when I did not go to a synagogue to be part of a *minyan,* I did not say *kaddish.*

Yet, on the days when I did not recite *kaddish,* I felt an emptiness and a longing; there was something missing from my mourning. For many reasons—not the least of which are centered in my own foibles and failings—I was still not motivated enough to go to the synagogue three times a day.

But, for all the reasons that the recitation of *kaddish* is worthy and worthwhile, soul-satisfying and inspiring, I wanted to say *kaddish* for my father. So, eventually, I gave myself permission to say *kaddish* alone—not as part of a *minyan,* not the midst of a community, not during a synagogue service, but by myself, alone.

This may seem to be a rather radical departure from Jewish law and custom, and, to some, may be in direct opposition to one of the most important reasons for saying *kaddish*. But this concept is not without precedent in the modern, liberal Jewish world.

When we moved out of the small villages and inner-city neighborhoods where the synagogues were close to our homes, we gave ourselves permission to drive to the synagogue on Shabbat and holidays. Even though traditional Jewish law prohibits riding on Shabbat, we declared it to be a greater good to come to the synagogue to pray along with our community than to stay home alone.

Here, too, we declare that when circumstance or choice inhibit praying with a *minyan*, it a greater good to say *kaddish* alone, than to not say *kaddish* at all.

At first, I found myself saying *kaddish* on a regular schedule, as if I were going to the three-times-a-day synagogue services. But, soon, I found myself saying *kaddish* whenever and wherever I was moved to honor and remember.

Yet, my solitary, personal *kaddish*-saying needed a perspective, a context. It needed what our sages call a *haskamah,* an imprimatur, a *kavannah,* a clearly articulated spiritual intention.

So, I composed this *kavannah,* this Spiritual Intention for saying *kaddish* alone. In language, litany, and rhythms of traditional Jewish prayer, and with envisionings and allusions that are intended to evoke familiar, comfortable images in the world of Jewish spirit, the *kavannah* first asks Heavenly and Angelic Beings to be with me, to make a *minyan,* a community of both Earth and Heaven. Then, it speaks words of love and blessing directly to the soul of my beloved deceased—acknowledging the reality of Earthly death; releasing the soul with love and blessing; and assuring the soul of God's sheltering love. Finally, it speaks directly to God, bringing my humble yet heartfelt *kaddish*-words of gratitude and praise.

It is still good to say *kaddish* in community, for in community there is history, and energy, and mutual responsibility, and unity, and friendship, and comfort, and love.

But, for those times when circumstance or choice keep you from being with a *minyan* to recite *kaddish,* this *kavannah* can serve as the prologue for saying *kaddish* by yourself.

If you wish to take this *kavannah* into the public arena, it can also be a very powerful prelude to the recitation of *kaddish* at the dedication of the gravestone, and at the yearly *yahrzeit.*

As well, it can bring focus and spiritual energy to the collective recitation of *kaddish* at the four-time-a-year Yiskor services, and every time the community gathers to say *kaddish* for those who died sanctifying God's holy Name.

I hope that this *kavannah* may be "the words of your mouth and the meditation of your heart," as you honor those who have gone to the Great Beyond. With you, I pray that their memories will be an everlasting benediction and a continuing inspiration.

KAVANNAH BEFORE KADDISH

(particularly when saying Kaddish *alone)*

In the Name of God, Source of All Being:
I call upon the Heavenly Hosts,
    who surround the Place of Glory;
And I call upon the Archangels,
    who fashion and shape the universe;
And I call upon the Angels,
    who serve the Divine will;
And I call upon the Guides and the MasterGuides,
    who watch over me and protect me;
And I ask you All:
    Be with me now,
    and give power to my words.

In the Name of God, Source of All Becoming:
I say to my *(choose one or more)* holy / revered / beloved /
    devoted / sweet . . .

_____

father, mother, brother, sister, son, daughter, husband, wife

_____

name

In every place and in every space in this great Cosmos,
it is known and revealed that you have left your Earthly body
and this physical world.
God has called you Home.
I remain ever-glad and ever-grateful for the Divine-gift of your life,
and though my heart still yearns for your physical presence,
with love, with honor, and with blessing,
I give you back to God, and release you to eternity.

I celebrate your soul-journey to the Light—
to that awesome place of
revelation and knowing,
of redemption and salvation,
of peace and harmony,
of grace, and compassion, and infinite love.
I am comforted and enheartened knowing that you dwell
in God's Sheltering Presence,
immersed in God's Holy Spirit.
For, with God,
it is safe, and sweet, and good.

To the Name of God, Source of All Blessing:
I come before You at that most sacred and wondrous place
where Heaven and Earth touch.
I stand with all those of the Divine Assembly,
and with all who desire to do holy work,
to speak these words that echo through there, and here, and everywhere,
through then, and now, and forever;
these words of hope and promise,
transformation, and evolution,
faith and love.

To You, O God,
I speak these ancient and ageless words
of praise and glory,
to Your Great and Holy Name.

WD

KADDISH

יִתְגַּדַּל וְיִתְקַדַּשׁ שְׁמֵהּ רַבָּא בְּעָלְמָא דִּי־בְרָא כִרְעוּתֵהּ,

Yit·ga·dal ve·yit·ka·dash she·mei ra·ba be·al·ma di·ve·ra chi·re·u·tei,

וְיַמְלִיךְ מַלְכוּתֵהּ בְּחַיֵּיכוֹן וּבְיוֹמֵיכוֹן וּבְחַיֵּי דְכָל־בֵּית

ve·yam·lich mal·chu·tei be·cha·yei·chon u·ve·yo·mei·chon u·ve·cha·yei de·chol beit

יִשְׂרָאֵל, בַּעֲגָלָא וּבִזְמַן קָרִיב, וְאִמְרוּ: אָמֵן.

Yis·ra·eil, ba·a·ga·la u·vi·ze·man ka·riv, ve·i·me·ru: a·mein.

יְהֵא שְׁמֵהּ רַבָּא מְבָרַךְ לְעָלַם וּלְעָלְמֵי עָלְמַיָּא.

Ye·hei she·mei ra·ba me·va·rach le·a·lam u·le·al·mei al·ma·ya.

יִתְבָּרַךְ וְיִשְׁתַּבַּח, וְיִתְפָּאַר וְיִתְרוֹמַם וְיִתְנַשֵּׂא, וְיִתְהַדָּר

Yit·ba·rach ve·yish·ta·bach, ve·yit·pa·ar ve·yit·ro·mam ve·yit·na·sei, ve·yit·ha·dar

וְיִתְעַלֶּה וְיִתְהַלַּל שְׁמֵהּ דְּקוּדְשָׁא, בְּרִיךְ הוּא, לְעֵלָּא מִן־כָּל־

ve·yit·a·leh ve·yit·ha·lal she·mei de·ku·de·sha, be·rich hu, le·ei·la min kol

בִּרְכָתָא וְשִׁירָתָא, תֻּשְׁבְּחָתָא וְנֶחֱמָתָא דַּאֲמִירָן בְּעָלְמָא,

bi·re·cha·ta ve·shi·ra·ta, tush·be·cha·ta ve·ne·che·ma·ta, da·a·mi·ran be·al·ma,

וְאִמְרוּ: אָמֵן.

ve·i·me·ru: a·mein.

יְהֵא שְׁלָמָא רַבָּא מִן־שְׁמַיָּא וְחַיִּים עָלֵינוּ וְעַל־כָּל־יִשְׂרָאֵל,

Ye·hei she·la·ma ra·ba min she·ma·ya ve·cha·yim a·lei·nu ve·al kol Yis·ra·eil,

וְאִמְרוּ: אָמֵן.

ve·i·me·ru: a·mein.

עֹשֶׂה שָׁלוֹם בִּמְרוֹמָיו, הוּא יַעֲשֶׂה שָׁלוֹם עָלֵינוּ וְעַל־כָּל־

O·seh sha·lom bi·me·ro·mav, hu ya·a·seh sha·lom a·lei·nu ve·al kol

יִשְׂרָאֵל, וְאִמְרוּ: אָמֵן.

Yis·ra·eil, ve·i·me·ru: a·mein.

THE LORD'S PRAYER

Most of the days of your life, you will not be in mourning; you will not be saying *kaddish* for a deceased loved One.

Yet, you still want to praise God. And, as a vehicle for that praise, the words and the rhythm of *kaddish* still resonate deeply within your soul.

Is there some way to say *kaddish* without saying the specific prayer that is reserved for the times you are in mourning?

As odd as it may seem to most Jews, the perfect prayer that reflects *kaddish* is what is known as "The Lord's Prayer."

This prayer is wholly associated with Christianity, where it is one of the central recitations.

Yet, there is not one word in the prayer that Jews cannot accept and embrace.

And it is no wonder. Like *kaddish*, "The Lord's Prayer" is a doxology—a prayer of high and great praise to God. It and *kaddish* are rooted in the same time period—about 2,000 years ago. Its sentiments and its rhythm are the same: *Kaddish: Yitgadal v'yitkadash Sh'mei rabbah.*" "Magnified and sanctified is (God's) Great Name."

The Lord's Prayer: "Our Father who art in Heaven, hallowed by Thy Name."

So, if you wish to express the sentiments in *kaddish* without saying *kaddish*, you can recite "The Lord's Prayer."

We leave the words in their traditional form, acknowledging the majesty of old English. You may be more comfortable addressing God with "You," and "Your," instead of "Thy" and "Thine."

You also may be more comfortable addressing God as "Father-Mother," or "Parent," or, simply, "God," or any other name that evokes the image for you. And—in the spirit of this personal 20 MINUTE KABBALAH practice—you may want to address God in the first person, saying "My," instead of "Our, " "me," instead of "us," and "I," instead of "we."

Begin with this little *kavannah,* this spiritual intention:

> *I—along with the souls of all sentient Beings—dedicate*
> *this prayer to my spiritual consciousness and my spiritual*
> *evolution, to open the flow of Divine energy in me*
> *and in the world.*

Then say:

> Our Father who art in Heaven,
> Hallowed be Thy Name.
> Thy Kingdom come,
> Thy will be done,
> on Earth
> as it is in Heaven.
> Give us this day
> our daily bread.
> And forgive us our trespasses,
> as we forgive those
> who trespass against us.
> And lead us not into temptation,
> but deliver us from evil
> For Thine is the Kingdom and the power and the glory
> forever and ever.
> Amen.

זָכוֹר —*Zachor*

RE-MEMBER

When you return from your journey into the world of Spirit, in order to best remember your encounter and your conversation with God, recite this little prayer.

Stand, with your arms at your sides, palms facing forward
and say:

"I now have 100% desire
that I am open and clear,
to receive the wisdom I have lived,
in all times and spaces."

Touch your wrists together
(as though hands are in a praying position)
and spread your hands slightly apart
(as though hands are in a catching position)
and say:

"In Sacred Light."

—brought down by ELKD

THE SEAL

BEING ONE

with

GOD,

THE UNIVERSE,

EACH OTHER,

YOUR GODSELF

When you come from being with God, you are infused with God's love. You are filled with peace.

You want that feeling to last for as long as possible. You want the love and peace that is in your heart to be manifest in your every word and deed. You want your voice of peace and love to be heard by the whole world.

The seal—the coda—of 20 MINUTE KABBALAH is the chant, *Shalom*—Peace.

The root word of *shalom* is *shalem,* which means whole, complete. Peace comes only when hearts and souls are whole.

Peace—in our hearts and our homes, in our land and in our world—is our greatest prayer and our most fervent desire.

Just imagine what would happen if, at the very same time, every human being on Earth prays for peace.

At that moment, there will be no hating, no enmity, no fighting, no war.

At that moment, the world will be whole.

There will be peace!

Your song of peace comes out of the UnManifest into the Void, is co-created by you and God into reality, and becomes spirit in matter and matter in spirit.

It flows out on the Love Vibration, fills the whole universe, and echoes through eternity.

Chant:

שָׁלוֹם

Shalom

Whole.

Complete.

Peace.

SKY BLUE:
ABOVE AND BELOW

◆———————

From the memory of an old childhood game comes the image of "Sky Blue"—the place, the pinnacle, of ultimate perfection.

Sky Blue is the ever-possible reality of the messianic vision of a world of decency and dignity, justice and righteousness, goodness and peace, light and love.

Your daily 20 MINUTE KABBALAH spiritual practice spirals you to the place where, in partnership with God, you are the healer and the transformer. You fashion the holy—and joyous—presence of Eden on Earth once again.

To celebrate your place in God's holy presence,
to rejoice in God Within you,
to affirm the deepest love that you and God share,
to pro-claim the Oneness of God, and of all God's worlds and creations,
to hasten your return to the Paradise of Eden on Earth,
every time it feels right and good, say these words:

I Am holding fast to the Tree of Life,
and safely journeying on Her pleasant paths.

I Am ready and prepared to open my heart fully
to the Eternal Heart.

I Am in perfect Oneness with my soul.

I Am in perfect Love.

I Am in readiness to be in the Garden of Eden.

Be blessed.
And be a blessing.

◆————————◆

To learn how you can bring

continuing Kabbalah-learning and practice

into your life,

please visit the website

www.20MinuteKabbalah.com

◆————————◆

AND NOW

---

1. STAY WITH GOD

When Moses came down the mountain, he was bathed in God's Light; he was beaming with God's Light. That holy Light reflected onto everyone Moses met.

When you "come down the mountain" from your conversation with God, how do you sustain the glorious feeling of being "in the Light," in God's holy presence?

Stay with God.

The Jewish tradition is to say 100 blessings a day.

St. Paul taught, "Pray always."

The Chasidic Rebbe Nachman of Bratslav said, "Pray. Pray. Pray."

100 blessings a day? Pray always? Pray, pray, pray?

How is that possible? There would not be time for anything else.

Metaphoric though it may be, that, of course, is the point.

If you say a blessing now, and know that you are to say a blessing five minutes from now; if you pray now, and know that you are soon to be praying again, then, you stay with God, and God stays with you. In constant God-energy, it is hard to say an unkind word, to be discourteous, to cheat in business, to tell a lie. For, when you are with God, and God is with you, you are certainly aware of God's word; you continue to do God's will.

When you pray always, when you say 100 blessings a day, you stay in the flow of God's design; you stay at-One with God. You stay in your own God-ing and your own God-ness.

So, be with God not only in your daily 20 minute meditation, but as much as you can. Stay in God-energy; stay in God's Light and Love for as long as you can. Eventually, every moment can be a God moment.

Be like Moses: Be beamed with God's Light, and become a beam of God's Light. Then, reflect God's Light to everyone you meet.

2. EXTEND THE PRACTICE

20 MINUTE KABBALAH is designed—no surprise—to take 20 minutes a day. And we think that you will need the full 20 minutes in order to chant your way through the *sefirot* of the Spiral Tree of Life, and to spend a few minutes in conversation with God. And, we know from other 20 minute spiritual practices that 20 minutes is a good amount of time to go into deep meditation, but not too much time so that you become distracted or weary.

Yet, do not feel wedded to or limited by the 20 minute structure. When you are in deep connection and communication with God, time does not exist. Do not "look at your watch," or count your minutes, thinking that you must finish your spiritual journey in 20 minutes. Stay with God for as long as it feels good and right.

Any day that your practice exceeds the usual 20 minutes, it is because that is exactly what you and God need on that day.

You can also extend your 20 MINUTE KABBALAH spiritual practice by doing it twice a day—once in the morning, once in the evening; the two most natural times for contemplation, prayer, and meditation.

And, you will likely find yourSelf chanting one or more of the *sefirot* chants at various times during the day. A chant will often bubble up from your unconscious. You may sing it or hum it without even realizing it, or without being aware of what *sefirah* chant you are singing.

Why this one and not that one? Why this one now, and that one later? Your heart and soul have chosen the exact words, or meanings, or energy that you need at that moment. It may be that those words or melody are what you need to say to God right then; it may be that you need to listen, because God is speaking those words and melodies to you right then. Or, it may be that those are the precise words—please open your heart to hear this, because this is deep—that God needs to hear right then, and you, God's precious child, sing them to the Divine.

The spiral ever spirals.

3. STAY WITH THE PRACTICE

Even the most soul-satisfying and exhilarating experiences and practices can go through "dry spells," becoming stale, and rote, and, yes, boring.

Even the most precious and loving relationships can hit the "troubled waters" of ennui, disinterest, distrust, and, yes, emptiness.

When your 20 MINUTE KABBALAH practice feels old and tired—and that is sure to happen now and then; when your relationship with God feels dispirited and hollow—and that, too, is sure to happen now and then, don't give up.

The great modern sage and conscience of our generation, Elie Wiesel teaches that you can be disappointed in God, you can be angry at God, you can wrestle and struggle with God, but you cannot ignore God—and, by extension, the spiritual practice that gets you to God.

Oh, how easy it would be to be "too tired," or "too busy," or "too hesitant" to keep up your daily 20 MINUTE KABBALAH spiritual practice because you "don't feel like it;" or it seems to be "accomplishing nothing."

But, if you give up, it will never accomplish anything.

Keva—the fixed order of the traditional prayer structure—exists to move you to spiritual intent, even when you don't feel it. Here, the spiral order of 20 MINUTE KABBALAH exists to bring you to spiritual intent, even when you may not feel it. Out of your *keva* comes your *kavannah.*

Never give up.

Keep doing your 20 MINUTE KABBALAH spiritual practice, whatever the circumstance, whatever the situation, whatever your mood, whatever your feelings. And *kavannah,* your spiritual intent, will prevail. Magic *will* bubble up.

Your love affair with God—and the responses to your heart's desires—will return and continue.

4. STAY WITH COMMUNITY

Judaism is a communal religion; the Jewish people are deeply connected.

There is great power, and energy, and mutual responsibility, and unity, and friendship in community. There is great beauty in joining together in prayer, in supporting prophetic-like causes of social justice, and in doing acts of lovingkindness for those who need your heart and your hands.

Some prayers—for example the haunting Kol Nidre chant on the eve of Yom Kippur—beg to be recited with others who feel the same historical connections and deep emotional response. In, for example, collecting food for the hungry, there is power in numbers. You can give ten cans of food; your community can give thousands. In loving and supporting our Land of Israel, your contribution is most worthy; added together with thousands and thousands of others, it holds formidable clout.

This 20 MINUTE KABBALAH is your personal prayer, your own way of being in intimate relationship with God. Yet, it is not license to become a monk or a hermit; it is not license to isolate or separate yourself from your community.

If you wonder what it might be like to be in deep personal prayer in the midst of other pray-ers, perhaps you might introduce this 20 MINUTE KABBALAH spiritual practice to your rabbi, your synagogue, your prayer-group, your *chavurah*, your *minyan*, your community. It can become a part of, or an addition to, a regular prayer service, giving individuals within the midst of a large group a new kind of opportunity for personal prayer. Or it can be the basis for an alternative worship experience, sponsored and endorsed—and, eventually, explored—by the community.

Yet, if your community is unwilling to explore 20 MINUTE KABBALAH—change is scary—then, continue your own daily spiritual practice, but do not withdraw from the communal journey. Stay with your community. And trust that the community will stay with you emotionally—supporting, encouraging, and celebrating your personal spiritual quest. The community needs you; you need community.

"All Israel is responsible, one for another."

This 20 MINUTE KABBALAH spiritual practice is a only a tiny taste of the beauty and the richness of Judaism and the numerous Jewish pathways to being in relationship with God.

Once you are deeply engaged in this daily spiritual journey, your interest may be sparked in other ways that Judaism can enrich your life, and bring you deeper soul-satisfaction.

5. STUDY AND LEARN

If you are not yet comfortable with Hebrew, you may want to learn a little of the "holy language," so that you can better understand the words you chant in your spiritual practice, and so that, in the words of our Reb Zalman, you can "break the *sefer* barrier"—you can have the key that unlocks the treasures of Jewish texts.

You may want to become familiar with the prayerbook, so that you know the traditional structure of prayer, and how the Spiral Tree of Life honors that structure, even as it "re-Jew-venates" and re-energizes it.

There is so much great wisdom in Judaism's sacred texts—the Bible, the *Talmud,* the *Midrash,* the *Zohar,* the Chasidic teachings. Most fortunate is this generation, for most all of Judaism's sacred texts and many of the commentaries have been translated into English. (While some classic Jewish texts were translated into widely-prevailing Yiddish, even in the glory days of Spanish, Eastern European, and Russian Jewry, few Jewish texts were ever translated into the languages of those countries.) So, even if you do not know Hebrew, you now have English-language access to Judaism's great books. We are in a true Golden Age of the possibility of Jewish learning.

When you delve into these texts, you learn Jewish history, and law, and legend.

You can understand the social, cultural, societal, political, religious, and spiritual elements of the ages. See what your ancestors sought; what they needed, what they asked, what they hoped. Understand their questions, their doubts, their yearnings. See the seedlings of their spiritual intent, the development of their faith and their religious communities. Even more, see how your ancestors encounter God throughout the generations.

Then, taking the experiences and insights of the past, the vastness and the richness of ever-continuing commentary and interpretation, you will mix the "seventy faces of Torah" with your own intuitive knowing, to deepen and broaden your own encounter—your own relationship—with God.

That is why the ancient sage taught, "Study Torah [in its sense of being the totality of Jewish learning] for everything is contained in it; constantly examine it, grow old and gray over it . . . for there is nothing more excellent than it."

When you open a *sefer*, a sacred book, and immerse your-Self in its teachings, time and time again, you will experience incredibly exciting "ah-ha" moments of recognition and real-ization. Through the prism of the truth of your *Da'at*, the wisdom of the ages is now yours. You are the receiver and, now you are the transmitter. The continuing revelation of God's word and will comes to you and through you.

There are two cautions: First, do not leave your study and learning to whim or chance. As the sages teach, "Set a fixed time for study," lest you never find the time for study.

And, then: Don't get so deeply into your head that you forget or ignore your heart. "God"—whom you meet every-day in the intimacy of your personal conversation—"desires the heart."

6. DO RITUALS

Religious rituals are symbols, touchstones, acts, that join and unify you with God, and link you to the history and the prac-tices of your people.

They bring beauty and meaning to existence. They make the ordinary holy, and the everyday sacred.

Even more, they go to the deepest places in the psyche, for they are without words, before words. They are the felt-sense that goes beyond the intellect into intuitive knowing.

Jewish rituals connect you to your ancestors and to your children's children—in homes and lands you cannot even begin to imagine. They merge you with the rhythms of the Jewish year, the Jewish cycles of celebration. They put the Jewish language on your lips, and Jewish identity in your being.

Say a *bracha*, a blessing. Cover your head in humility. Wrap in the fringes. Hear the sound of the *shofar*. Dwell in the *succah*. Shake the *lulav*. Eat the *matzah*. Mourn for the destruction. Bewail the exile. Dance with the Torah.

And, especially, invite Shabbat into your life.

God created, and, on the seventh day, God rested.

You co-create with God, and, every seventh day, you can rest.

You can carve out one day a week—or a few dedicated minutes or hours on that day—to rest your physical body, to reinvigorate your mind, to revive and restore your spirit, to renew your soul.

Your Shabbat practice may be a traditional 25 hour observance. Or, you may choose to attend synagogue services on Friday evening and/or Shabbat morning. Or, you may spend just thirty seconds lighting the Shabbat candles, to make the day different from all others. Or, you may choose an especially delicious rendition of your 20 MINUTE KABBALAH practice; perhaps once on Friday evening, and then again on Saturday morning.

However you choose to observe Shabbat, you are lifted up beyond your everyday world. You are given a glimpse, a taste, of what the world will be when *Masheachvelt*, the messianic time of harmony and peace comes to this world—when you and God have co-created Paradise on Earth.

As Reb Shlomo *zt"l* teaches, "One day, one day, the whole world will be Shabbas."

Be with God on the weekly anniversary of God's—and your—acts of creation and rest.

7. DO MITZVOT

All of Jewish life, all of Jewish lifestyle has one purpose: to teach you and to inspire you to a life of right and of good; of high moral behavior and pristine character.

Be with God by living God's ethical values.

Honor your parents. Feed the hungry. Be honest in business. Be kind to the stranger. Welcome the guest. Be humble. Be modest. Be gracious. Tell the truth. Have compassion. Balance justice with mercy. Love your neighbor. Rise up before the elders. Heal the sick. Dower the bride. Comfort the mourner. Meet the needs of the community. Share the work of your hands. Do social justice. Celebrate the decency, and the dignity, and the human rights of every human being. Do *tikkun*—heal, balance, and transform the shattered broken-ness in hearts and homes.

Pursue peace.

Bring harmony.

Build a perfect world.

8. LOVE THE LAND

The Jewish connection to the Land of Israel is ancient and deep; unyielding and ever-continuing. "God, Torah, and Israel—the Land and the people—are One."

"This is the land which I have promised your ancestors."

"From out of Zion the Law shall go forth, and the voice of God from Jerusalem."

"And we will worship God on the Holy Mountain. *Yerushalayim, Yerushalayim*—Jerusalem, Jerusalem."

"We have come to the land to build it and to be built by it."

Israel is the heart of the Jewish people, the soul of humankind, and the spirit of God.

Jerusalem is the place where Heaven and Earth meet—where the glory of God and the greatness of God's children become One.

"For Zion's sake, I will not be silent, for the sake of Jerusalem, I will not be still, until her triumph emerges radiant."

Be with God by treasuring God's Promised Land, God's Holy Land.

9. HEAR. SEE. DREAM.

Be with God by being constantly aware of God.

God's "signs and wonders" manifest everywhere, always.

God's messages come to you not only when you are with God in prayer and meditation, but all the time.

Attune your hearing. God will tell you.

Sharpen your seeing. God will show you.

And God will "dream into you" by day and by night.

Remember: no less than Moses, or Jeremiah, or Elijah, you are a prophet. As God came to them, God comes to you.

You just have to be open. You just have to be ever-ready.

Ask to be a channel, and God will flow through you.

10. GET A TEACHER

When you delve into the teachings of Jewish spirituality and mysticism, you need a teacher to bring you into the depths.

Find a wise teacher who knows text, and can guide you to the deepest learning.

But, even more, find a spiritual guide, who will be God's partner in taking you to the depths of your soul.

You need a Rebbe—stripped of all ego; who will strip you of all ego—who will accompany you on the mystical pathways, journeying to God.

You need a Rebbe who can look into your eyes, and see into your soul; who will see your own Rebbe-ness within you, and guide you to the heights, and the depths, and the holiness of your being.

You may not always like what your Rebbe tells you; you may not always be comfortable when your Rebbe confronts or challenges you. But, you will always be sure that your Rebbe loves you.

11. MEET YOUR SPIRIT GUIDES

You have Angels, and Guides, and MasterGuides, who are with you on your journey through life.

The members of your Guidance Team are God's loyal and affectionate servants.

They are with you to boost your skills, talents, and God-given gifts; to help you fulfill your mission and your purpose here on this Earth; and to smooth the pathways when you journey to God.

The members of your Guidance Team adore you. They cherish, and honor, and love you.

Come to know them, gladly accept their service to you, and revel in their devotion to you.

12. GET A SPIRIT BUDDY

Even with a teacher, even with a Rebbe, even with your own Guides, it can be a continual challenge to maintain your 20 MINUTE KABBALAH practice, to enter into the world of Spirit everyday.

So, get a Spirit Buddy—a friend, a companion, who, like you, is a 20 MINUTE KABBALAH practitioner.

Be a listening ear to each other. Encourage each other. Support each other. Reassure each other. Inspire each other. Rejoice with each other.

If you and your spouse, partner, or significant other are both doing the 20 MINUTE KABBALAH practice each day, you can serve as each other's Spirit Buddy.

But, it may be even more beneficial to have a Spirit Buddy who is not an intimate, but who can be an objective observer and cheerleader.

Choose a Spirit Buddy, and use the form on the next page to exchange information, so that you can know how and when to be in touch with each other.

Your Spirit Buddy may become your "new best friend," and—as we have witnessed a number of times—your life-long best friend.

When you look into the face, or hear the voice of your Spirit Buddy, you are looking at the face and hearing the voice of God. For, God is in you; God is in your Spirit Buddy. You reflect God's Light to each other.

My
20 MINUTE KABBALAH
Spirit buddy
is:

Name _____

Spouse / Partner Name _____

Child(ren)'s Name(s) and age(s) _____

_____

Address _____

_____

Phones Home _____ Cell _____

        Work _____

E-Mail _____

My Spirit Buddy and I have agreed that we can be in touch with each other:

___ at home

    ___ weekdays (beginning at ____ am)

    ___ weekday evenings (from ____ pm, until ____ pm)

    ___ weekend days (from ____ am, until ____ pm)

    ___ weekend evenings (from ____ pm, until ____ pm)

___ at work

    ___ during work hours ___ only during breaks and lunch time

13. EVOLVE AND TRANSFORM

We have been given this 20 MINUTE KABBALAH for this moment in time.

As you go deeper and deeper into this spiritual practice, the practice itself may change and evolve for you, for it will enter into the Back of your *Da'at,* and, eventually emerge from the Front of your *Da'at,* viewed through your own prism and shaped by your own truth—and by the constantly unfolding truths of the universe.

Within these neo-Kabbalistic-Chasidic mystical pathways, you and God will find and be with each other in your own intimate, unique dance.

And all is well.

We imagine, then, that, before long, there will be "Orthodox" 20 MINUTE KABBLAH and "Reform" 20 MINUTE KABBALAH. Then, wanting to retain some of what has been changed, there will be "Conservative" 20 MINUTE KABBALAH. Then, there will be "Reconstructed" 20 MINUTE KABBALAH and, ultimately, "Renewing" 20 MINUTE KABBALAH.

And the journey to God will continue to unfold just as it should.

Evolution and Transformation.

You and the Living God in organic, ever-emerging, ever-growing, ever-loving relationship.

And all is perfect.

Shalom—Fare Well

Through 20 MINUTE KABBALAH you stand at the Bush—which always burns; you walk through the Gates—which are always open.

You spiral through the mystical pathways of the Spiral Tree of Life. You meet God.

You are with God everyday—every moment, if you wish—in sweet surrender, in the holy talk of intimate love.

As taught by the holy Baal Shem Tov—the father of Chasidut, who built upon the living fountainhead of the Kabbalists—you can be a living embodiment of *Adam Kadmon*—the first human being, the repository of all souls.

You can be Above and Below—a human being of flesh and blood, and an elevated soul, all at the same time.

You can be the foundation of faith, and love, and goodness in this world and for worlds yet to come.

So, whenever it feels right and good—as often as you wish, and in as many repetitions as you wish—say:

"Return me unto You, O God,

and I will return.

Renew my days

as at the very, very beginning."

◆

To learn how you can bring

continuing Kabbalah-learning and practice

into your life,

please visit the website

www.20MinuteKabbalah.com

◆

To invite

RABBI WAYNE DOSICK

to lead a

20 MINUTE KABBALAH

Workshop,

or to invite him to be

Scholar-in-Residence

at your synagogue, church, or in your community,

email: Dosick@20Minute Kabbalah.com

or call

1-877 SOUL KID

EndPiece I
20 MINUTE KABBALAH
ON THE GO

Here is a summary version of 20 MINUTE KABBALAH,
to photocopy, and take with you wherever you go.

Energy Balance

A Prayer for Standing at the Burning Bush

Coming into the World of Spirit

1. TIFERET — THE HEART SPACE
Coming Into God's Holy Presence

שִׁוִּיתִי הֹ׳ לְנֶגְדִי תָמִיד

Shiviti Adonai L'negdi Tamid

I place God before me always.

2. GEVURAH — THE PLACE OF INGATHERING & BOUNDARIES
Coming Into God's Protection

וְשַׁבְתִי בְּבֵית הֹ׳

V'shavti b'veit Adonai

I place mySelf in God's care.

3. CHESED — THE PLACE OF BOUNDLESS OUTREACHING
Feeling God's Love

חֵן וָחֶסֶד וְרַחֲמִים

Chen, Va'Chesed, V'Rachamim

Grace, and Love, and ComPassion

4. NETZACH — THE PLACE OF OUTWARD CREATIVE ENERGY
Toning the Vibration of God's Love

קָדוֹשׁ קָדוֹשׁ קָדוֹשׁ

Kadosh, Kadosh, Kadosh

Holy, Holy, Holy

5. HOD — THE PLACE OF INNER CREATIVE ENERGY
Becoming One With the Breath of God

רוח

Ruach

Spirit / Breath of God

6. BINAH — THE PLACE OF DIRECT, FELT-SENSE EXPERIENCE
Being God's Co-Creative Partner

ברוך שאמר והיה העולם

Baruch She'amar v'hayah haOlam

**Praised is the One Who spoke,
and the World came to be.
Praised is the One.**

7. CHOCHMAH — THE PLACE OF CONSCIOUS INTELLIGENCE
Co-Creating God's Worlds

הנשמה לך

והגוף פעלך

חוסה על עמלך

HaNeshamah Lach

V' ha goof pa-aLach

Chusah al ahmaLach

**You created my soul,
And my body, too
Please God, Please God,
Have compassion with me.**

8. YESOD — THE LIFE FORCE
Manifesting God's Design

שׁוֹמֵעַ תְּפִילָה

Sho'me-ah tefilah

O, please God,
Please listen.
Please listen,
Listen to my prayer.

9. THE BACK OF DA'AT — THE ENTRANCE INTO GOD'S TIME TUNNEL, AT THE HIGH HEART
Coming Into Perfect Alignment With God

אֶהְיֶה אֲשֶׁר אֶהְיֶה

Eh-yeh Asher Eh-yeh

I Am, I Am, I Am That I Am

10. MALCHUT — also known as the *sefirah* of the SHECHINAH — THE INDWELLING FEMININE MANIFEST MATERIALITY
Being in Oneness With God

שְׁמַע יִשְׂרָאֵל ה׳ אֱלֹהֵינוּ ה׳ אֶחָד

Sh'ma Yisrael Adonai Elohenu Adonai Echad

Listen, all People!
The Lord is our God.
The Lord is One.

11. KETER—THE DWELLING PLACE OF GOD & THE UNION WITH GOD; THE PLACE WHERE MATTER AND SPIRIT MEET, WHERE MATTER BECOMES SPIRIT
Communicating with God

הִנֵּנִי

Hineini

Here I Am

12. THE FRONT OF DA'AT—THE EMERGING FROM GOD'S TIME TUNNEL, WITH NEW-FOUND TRUTH AT THE HIGH HEART
Ever-Experiencing God and GodSelf

אָנֹכִי

Anochi

I

זָכוֹר —*Zachor* RE-MEMBER

"I now have 100% desire
that I am open and clear,
to receive the wisdom I have lived,
in all times and spaces."

Seal—BEING ONE

שָׁלוֹם

Shalom

EndPiece II
QUESTIONS TO CONSIDER
IN YOUR
BOOK OF GOD

TIFERET

1. What does it feel like to "live in" the Heart?

   now that I am aware that I am there?

   in the next few hours?

   each new day?

2. How do I think about / see / envision God?

3. How do I "place God before me always"?

   How do I "shut out" the distractions when they keep me away from God?

4. What Name am I most comfortable calling God?

    Does that change according to my mood, my need, how I am feeling in relationship to God?

5. How does it feel to be in connection with God?

    How does it feel on the days when I do not sense the connection?

    How does it feel on the days when I sense the "re-connection" after having been "disconnected" for a while?

GEVURAH

1. What does *Gevurah's* feminine strength of ingathering and sheltering feel like to me?

   How do I imagine it feels to someone of the opposite gender?

2. How do I feel about boundaries and limitations—even ones that are alleged to be positive?

3. What is pure? What is impure?

   What does it mean to me to require pure space for my encounter with God?

4. For me, what is God's protection, God's care?

   How does it feel to be in God's protection, God's care?

5. How do I establish pure and protected space for all my relationships?

6. How does God's protection and care feel different from the protection and care given by parents, spouse, and (in elder years) children, friends, employer, community, country?

   When I am the caregiver and protector, how can I be most God-like in my caring and protecting?

CHESED

1. What does *Chesed's* masculine boundless outreaching feel like to me?

   How do I imagine it feels to someone of the opposite gender?

2. How do I know, really, really know, that God loves me?

3 How do I move away from / counter the embedded image of the collective consciousness that God is a harsh, punishing God?

4. How do I open mySelf to receive God's grace, unconditional love, and compassion?

5. How do I affirm my worthiness to offer my own grace, unconditional love, and compassion to God?

6. How do I best perform acts of *chesed* to be with / best aid others in ComPassion—in their suffering?

7. How do I best be gentle with mySelf, to embrace my own grace, unconditional love, and compassion for mySelf?

NETZACH

1. What does the *Netzach*-male energy of expanse and increase feel like within me?

    How do I imagine it feels to someone of the opposite gender?

2. What do I imagine "angel energy" feels like for the angels?

    Since I am "just a little lower than the angels," what does "angel energy" feel like for me?

3. What does the Love Vibration look like / feel like to me?

4. What would a world "filled with God's glory" look like / feel like to me?

    to the world?

5. When I chant *Kadosh,* can I see where the Love Vibration is going, and reverberating, and echoing?

    What effect can I see / feel from the journey of the Love Vibration into all the spaces and places in the world?

HOD

1. What does the *Hod*-female energy of contraction and inner creativity feel like within me?

   How do I imagine it feels to someone of the opposite gender?

2. When I am especially mindful, can I feel and hear my breath within me?

   what does my breath sound like?

   how does it feel in my lungs? throughout my whole being?

3. Since my being is the Breath of God, how do I feel God Within?

4. Can I sense that God's Breath and my breath are not separate, but that God and I are breathing together in shared InBreaths and OutBreaths?

   How does it feel to share one breath with God?

5. How does it feel to sense my breath-purpose of sending the Love Vibration to all creation?

   How does the Love Vibration feel in every cell of my being?

   Can I imagine all the spaces and places that it is going?

6. How does it feel to be like a *Seraph,* the greatest of all Angels, standing at the side of God's Throne, having the Love Vibration flow through me?

BINAH

1. What does the *Binah*-female energy of felt-sense experience and intuitive knowing feel like to me?

   How do I imagine it feels to someone of the opposite gender?

2. Do I sense that "the Word" is enough to create worlds?

   If so, why isn't God's Word enough to have made a peaceful world?

   If not, how do I reconcile my thoughts / feelings about creation with the biblical account?

3. How do I "watch my words" so that they do good, not harm; so that they create, not destroy, in my many worlds?

4. How do I feel when I am in the Void?

5. How do I feel going into God's Void?

6. How do I feel being God's dancing partner?

7. How do I shape my words into worlds?

   How do I speak into being the kind of world I envision?

CHOCHMAH

1. What does the *Chochmah*-male energy of thoughtful wisdom feel like to me?

   How do I imagine it feels to someone of the opposite gender?

2. How do I best balance being a "feeling and thinking" person?

   How do I feel / react if one characteristic seems to dominate me?

3. What is "wisdom"? Am I wise?

   If I don't feel "wise" where do I attain wisdom?

4. How do I feel being a co-creator of worlds?

   Isn't that God's job? Why me?

5. How do I assure that God's Word—and mine—come into the world with the greatest of integrity?

6. How do I overcome my anxieties and my fears when I "send forth" (or "let go") that which I hold most precious out on its (his / her) own?

7. Why should I have to ask for God's compassion if I feel that I have earned and deserve it?

   How does it feel to ask God—the Fashioner of my being—for compassion, if I do not feel that I have earned it / deserve it?

8. How do I express / manifest "awe of God"?

YESOD

1. How well do I appreciate and "feed" my *Yesod*-life force?

2. How well do I balance my physical and spiritual worlds?

    What do I do when one seems to dominate the other?

3. How do I feel knowing that it is my prayer that calls something from the UnManifest into the Void and into creation?

    How does it feel knowing that my prayers calling from the UnManifest into the Void are always answered?

4. How well do I pray?

    How satisfying is my inner prayer-life?

    What can I do to enrich my praying and my prayers?

5. How do I feel knowing that God is dependent upon me for God's God-ness?

6. How do I feel when it seems as if God is not answering my prayers the way I would like?

7. How do I best understand God's plan for me, and how it fits into the universal plan?

THE BACK OF DA'AT

1. At the core of my being, do I feel in exile from Paradise?

    Does that loss create an existential loneliness within me that I always carry with me?

2. Like Moses, am I a reluctant prophet, or am I eager to accept God's mission for me?

    Am I completely willing to "show up"?

3. How does it feel to stand at the Burning Bush; to be ready to hear and see my as yet unknown mission?

4. How do I understand / feel the "I Am" presence of God— God's GodSelf?

5. How do I understand / feel my own "I Am" presence— my own GodSelf?

6. What is it like to be in *Da'at's* time Tunnel, with *emet,* the full truth of All That Is flowing through *Da'at,* and flowing through me?

7. Am I reluctant or eager to have *emet* shaped by my prism, and emerge as a new truth for the world?

    Do I feel ready and worthy?

    If not, how do I get ready and feel worthy?

MALCHUT

1. Is *Sh'ma Yisrael* ingrained in me as my declaration of faith?

   Do I recite it by rote, or do I pay attention to its words and meaning?

2. Am I comfortable using *Sh'ma Yisrael* as a mantra to connect with God?

3. Does the *Sh'ma Yisrael* mantra work for me? Does it help connect me with God?

4. How does it feel to me to move into God-space, God-energy?

5. How does it feel when God meets me in the physical, material word of Earth?

   Can I feel spirit in matter?

6. How do I relate to / am I comfortable with God who is "up there," and, at the same time, "down here"?

7. How does the *Shechinah*-manifesting-energy feel to me?

   Is it only theoretical, or can I really feel it inside my insides?

8. Do I feel the Oneness of All That Is—God, and me, and the universe?

KETER

1. Was I ready to say to God today, *"Hineini,* Here I Am"?

   Remembering that God is always ready for me, what is it that will make me better ready tomorrow?

2. How did I feel being with God today?

3. What did I say?

4. What did God respond?

5. For what did I ask today?

6. What did God respond?

7. What do I really, really want to know?

   How do I best ask?

8. Is there anything I didn't ask God today that I wanted to ask / that I forgot to ask / that I should have asked / that I was afraid to ask?

   How do I prepare to ask tomorrow?

THE FRONT OF DA'AT

1. How difficult was it for me today to come back from being with God?

2. How pleased am I to be fully back in my Earth-life?

   If I am not too pleased, how do I best recapture my love for life?

3. How has being with God today reshaped me?

   What mysteries and secrets do I now better understand and know?

4. Have the desires of my heart been heard?

5. How was my experience in the Time Tunnel of *Da'at?*

6. What new truths for the universe do I bring with me today?

   Is the world ready for my truth?

   If so, how do I give over my truth with grace and dignity?

   If not, how do I gently and forcefully enlighten?

7. How do I relate to God as *Anochi*—the totality of All That Is?

8. How do I nurture and grow *Anochi Within,* my GodSelf?

   the connection between *Anochi-God* and *Anochi-God Within?*

EndPiece III
KABBALAH
TEXTS & TEACHERS

———◆———

You may want to delve more deeply into the Jewish mystical tradition
by studying some of the original source texts, and by knowing the
teachings of some of the first sages and masters of Kabbalah.
Here is a very brief compendium of texts and teachers.
Fortunate is our generation that all these core writings are now
available in English translation.

TEXTS

The central text of the Kabbalah is the ***Zohar—The Book of Splendor.***

Tradition attributes the *Zohar* to the second-century rabbinic sage
Shimon bar Yochai. Modern scholarship argues that the real author is
Moses de Leon of Granada, Spain, writing in 1268 CE, who attempted
to make the reader think that bar Yochai was the writer, thus giving the
Zohar historical roots and authenticity.

Either way, beginning in the 13th century, the new Kabbalists
moved away from the rational—most championed by the 12th century sage Moses Maimonides—into the spiritual.

The *Zohar* traces the Jewish mystical tradition back to Abraham, further back to Adam and Eve, even further back to the moment of creation, and all the way back to the beginning before the beginning, to the word before the word.

The *Zohar* is a mystical commentary on the Torah. Its far-ranging topics include the nature of God; the structure of the universe; the nature of human souls, prayer, good and evil, sin and repentance; and the meaning of human existence.

There are a number of English translations currently available. The finest translation, along with copious, brilliant scholarly commentary, is being prepared volume by volume by Professor Daniel C. Matt. It is known as the Pritzker Edition of The Zohar.

Other classic texts of the Kabbalists include:

Sefer Yetzirah—The Book of Foundation, or Creation, written by an unknown author (although some attribute it to Abraham or Rabbi Akiba) at an unknown time (speculation ranges between biblical times and the 11th century CE—quite a range of possibility. Thus, it is considered by some to be a "pre-Kabbalistic" text.)

Sefer Yetzirah is a "little" text—1,300 words in the short version; 2,500 in the long—with "big" power. It tells of God and the act of creation; deepens the concept of the *sefirot;* outlines the purpose and the power of the 22 Hebrew letters; discusses both angels and astrology; and is said to contain hidden formulae for creating and manifesting.

Sefer HaBahir—The Book of Illumination—also of unknown authorship, first seen in Germany, and then in France in the 13th century. The Kabbalists attribute it to Rabbi Nehunah ben HaKana, a first century sage.

Sefer HaBahir, most agree, is the oldest of all Kabbalah texts; it is widely quoted in the *Zohar.* It introduces the concept of the 10 *sefirot,* and the 32 paths of wisdom. It concentrates on the mystical aspects of the Hebrew letters; and introduces to Jewish thought the idea of *gilgool hanefesh*, the "rolling," or transmigration, of souls—reincarnation.

Sefer Chasidim—The Book of the Disciples—brought Jewish mysticism into the Jewish mainstream in 13th century Germany. Although unrelated to the 18th century Chasidim (except for the similar name) the teachings here can be seen as foreshadowing the movement that would later grow up.

Sefer Chasidim reflects the concerns of the followers of a particular branch of the Jewish mystical tradition. It tells of the unity of God, and emphasizes the prophetic sense of social and economic justice.

Sefer Rezial HaMalach—The Book of Rezial the Angel—was, according to old Jewish legend, given by God to Adam in the Garden of Eden, making it the world's oldest book. It is often attributed to Eleazar of Worms (Germany) in the mid-13th century. The first preserved manuscript was published in Amsterdam in 1701.

Sefer Rezial HaMalach is a compilation of five books. It tells of the holy names of God; the divisions between Heaven and Hell; the names and hierarchies of the angels; and includes teachings on astronomy, astrology, and magical formulae.

TEACHERS

Abraham Abulafia (1240–1292) Spain, Israel, Italy, and Greece.
Best known for meditation "beyond the sense," particularly focusing on the Hebrew alphabet.

Joseph ben Abraham Gikatilla (1248–1325) Spain.
Best known for his idea on the hidden meaning of the Names of God. His most important work is *Sha'arei Orah—Gates of Light.*

Moses Cordovero (1522–1570) S'fat.

His thinking was influenced by Joseph Karo, author of the legal compendium, the *Shulchan Aruch,* and mystical liturgist, Solomon Alkabez.

Part of the school of S'fat mystics who identified with the *Shechinah* in exile by adopting rigid personal disciplines, moral purity, and ascetic practices such as *gerushin,* "banishments," isolating themselves for prayer, meditation, and study of esoteric subjects.

A prolific author, whose best known works are *Pardes Rimonim— Orchard of Pomegranates* and *Tomer Devorah—The Palm Tree of Deborah,* which is a code for moral and ethical behavior.

Isaac Luria (1534–1572) Jerusalem, Egypt, and S'fat. Known as HaAri, the Lion.

One of the most influential of all the S'fat Kabbalists—despite his death at age 38, and despite the fact that he left almost no writings.

His most important teachings revolve around: the contraction of God for the purpose of creation; personal morality; prayer as the pathway to God; the hidden meaning and secrets of Torah; and *gilgool hanefesh,* reincarnation.

Chaim Vital (1542–1620) S'fat, Jerusalem, and Damascus.

Luria's greatest disciple, who popularized and spread his master's teachings, and established the system of Lurianic Kabbalah.

His most important work is *Etz Chaim—The Tree of Life,* which is the source for the Lurianic teachings.

Judah Loew of Prague (1512–1609) Nikolsburg, Posen, and Prague.

Community rabbi, scholar, innovative thinker, and mystic, who was one of the early transitional figures between Kabbalah and Chasidut.

Best known for making the "Golem."

Moses Chaim Luzzato (1707–1747) Italy, Holland, Central Europe, Israel.

Educated in both religious and secular studies, he adopted Kabbalistic thinking, which made him a threat to the rabbis of Central Europe because of their fear that his mysticism might cause a revival of the pseudo-messianism of Shabbatai Zvi.

Author of *Mesilat Yesharim—The Path of the Upright* which avoids discussion of Kabbalistic mysticism, concentrating, instead, on a life of deep piety. The developing Chasidic movement considered this book as one of its main statements of purpose.

THE CHASIDIM

The Founder

Israel ben Eliezar, the Baal Shem Tov (The Besht) (1700–1760) Okup, Podolia, Ukraine, and Mezbizh, western Ukraine.

The Chasidim opened the teachings of the Kabbalah beyond the elite, learned scholar and the mystic, to include all people of (simple) piety. They expanded the pathway to God from Kabbalistic contemplative meditation to include fervent, joyous prayer, chant, and dance.

During the 18th, 19th, and early 20th century, many disciples of the Ba'al Shem—brilliant, charismatic teachers, and spiritual guides and healers, spread Chasidut into the cities, towns, villages and *shtetlach* of Eastern Europe, Russia, and Ukraine.

During the Shoah, the Holocaust of 1939–45, when more than six million Jews were murdered by the nazis, most Chasidic life—along with most Jewish life in Europe and Russia—was wiped out.

The "saving remnant" who survived, rebuilt a small but vibrant Chasidic life in Israel and the United States, and continue to influence new generations of Jews.

The Chasidim, with their deep spirit and worthy teachings, were—and continue to be—natural, and most worthy, successor-partners to the Kabbalists.

To obtain additional copies of

the 20 MINUTE KABBALAH CHANTS AUDIO CD

by download or on a disk,

and

To learn how you can bring

continuing Kabbalah-learning and practice

into your life,

please visit the website

www.20MinuteKabbalah.com

To invite

RABBI WAYNE DOSICK

to lead a

20 MINUTE KABBALAH

Workshop,

or to invite him to be

Scholar-in-Residence

at your synagogue, church, or in your community,

email: Dosick@20Minute Kabbalah.com

or call

1-877 SOUL KID

"I asked for wonder."

—*Abraham Joshua Heschel*

Permissions & Gratitudes

- Central Conference of American Rabbis for the transliterated *Kaddish* from *The New Union Prayerbook,* CCAR © 1975.

- Shoshana Cooper for her copyrighted melody to *"Shiviti,"* which is heard on the *20 Minute Kabblah Chants* Audio-CD

- Neilah Carlebach for Rabbi Shlomo Carlebach *zt"l* copyrighted melodies to *"Ruach"* and *"Shalom,"* which are heard on the *20 Minute Kabblah Chants* Audio-CD

- The *Harfu*/Be Still meditation for "Coming Into the World of Spirt" is adapted from *20 Minute Retreats: Revive Your Spirits in Just Minutes a Day with Simple-Self-Led Exercises,* Rachel Harris, Ph.D., An Owl Book, Henry Holt © 2000. We always marvel at how universal wisdom—especially that of the ancient psalmist—bubbles up in many diverse places at the same time.

ABOUT THE AUTHORS

RABBI WAYNE DOSICK, Ph.D, is the spiritual guide of The Elijah Minyan and the director of The Soul Center for Spiritual Healing. For more than sixteen years, he served on the faculty of the University of San Diego, and has written more than 400 articles for the *San Diego Jewish Times.* "Rabbinic Insights," his bi-weekly column of religious, political, and social commentary, can now be read at www.sdjewishworld.com. He is the award-winning author of seven previous books, including the now-classic, *Living Judaism: The Complete Guide to Jewish Belief, Tradition and Practice;* the visionary *Soul Judaism: Dancing with God into a New Era;* the deeply comforting and theologically ennobling, *When Life Hurts: A Book of Hope,* and the much beloved, *Golden Rules: The Ten Ethical Values Parents Need To Teach Their Children.*

ELLEN KAUFMAN DOSICK, MSW, with degrees from the University of Chicago, directed social service agencies, taught at the University of Southern California, and worked for decades as a clinical psychotherapist. She is now the world Master Practitioner and Teacher of the spiritual psychotherapy, Soul Memory Discovery. She is the author of the widely read internet publication, *Cosmic Times: Spiritual News you Can Use.* (www.soulmemorydiscovery.com.)

REB WAYNE & ELLEN are highly acclaimed international speakers and teachers who have lectured, and led seminars, workshops, and retreats, in a wide variety of settings.

Together, they are the authors of the pathfinding book, *Spiritually Healing the Indigo Children (and Adult Indigos, Too!): The Practical Guide and Handbook.*

They live in La Costa (north suburban San Diego) California, where their home is a center for learning, prayer, and healing; and is a gathering place for spiritual seekers.

ABOUT THE SINGER

CANTOR KATHY ROBBINS has served as the Cantor and Music Director of Temple Solel in Cardiff-by-the-Sea, California since 1984. She holds a B.A. in psychology from New York University, a M.Ed from the University of Texas, Austin, and Cantorial Certification from the Hebrew Union College-Jewish Institute of Religion. She recently completed the Cantorial Leadership Program of the Institute for Jewish Spirituality. Her creative contributions include a unique *Freilich Friday* Shabbat Evening service with her 6-piece band; a Mind-Body-Spirit Adult Education Wellness Wheel; and her soon-to-be-released CD *"Shavat Vayinafash: Contemporary Music for Shabbat Evening."* Cantor Robbins resides in Carlsbad, California with her husband and son.

כִּי ה׳ יִהְיֶה לָךְ לְאוֹר עוֹלָם

Ki Adonai yiyeh lach l'or olam

God shall be your Everlasting Light

—Isaiah 40:20